wheels of CHANGE

How Women Rode the Bicycle to Freedom

Wheels of

(With a Few Flat Tires Along the Way)

Change

sue macy

NATIONAL GEOGRAPHIC

WASHINGTON, D.C.

IN memory of Lou arnold, baseball pioneer,
who saw right through me and loved me anyway

PREPARED BY THE BOOK DIVISION

Nancy Laties Feresten, *Vice President,
Editor in Chief, Children's Books*

Jonathan Halling, *Design Director,
Children's Publishing*

Jennifer Emmett, *Executive Editor,
Reference and Solo, Children's Books*

Carl Mehler, *Director of Maps*

R. Gary Colbert, *Production Director*

Jennifer A. Thornton, *Managing Editor*

STAFF FOR THIS BOOK

Jennifer Emmett, *Editor*

James Hiscott, Jr., *Art Director*

Lori Epstein, *Illustrations Editor*

Marty Ittner, *Designer*

Kate Olesin, *Editorial Assistant*

Grace Hill, *Associate Managing Editor*

Lewis R. Bassford, *Production Manager*

Susan Borke, *Legal and Business Affairs*

MANUFACTURING AND
QUALITY MANAGEMENT

Christopher A. Liedel, *Chief Financial Officer*

Phillip L. Schlosser, *Vice President*

Chris Brown, *Technical Director*

Nicole Elliott, *Manager*

Rachel Faulise, *Manager*

Cover: Actress Madge Lessing trumpets the era of the bicycle in this photograph from 1898. Born in London, England, in 1866, Lessing performed frequently on the stages of London and Broadway and also acted in a number of early silent films. She died in 1932.

Title Page: Katharine Wright, second from right, and four friends are about to embark on a bicycle outing at Oberlin College in Ohio around 1898. Wright's brothers, Orville and Wilbur, were bicycle mechanics who would soon turn their attention to a new invention, the airplane.

Opposite: Detail from an advertising card for the New Brunswick Tire Company. See page 69 for the entire ad.

The Library of Congress cataloged the 2011 edition as follows:

Macy, Sue. Wheels of change : how women rode the bicycle to freedom
(with a few flat tires along the way) / by Sue Macy. p. cm. Includes
bibliographical references and index. ISBN 978-1-4263-0761-4 (hardcover
: alk. paper) -- ISBN 978-1-4263-0762-1 (library binding : alk. paper) 1.
Cycling for women--United States--History. I. Title. GV1057.M33 2011
796.6082--dc22   2010027141

2017 paperback edition ISBN: 978-1-4263-2855-8

contents

foreword

Bicycles have long played a role in my life. As a young woman, I rode one year-round before I had a car. But it was later in adulthood that the bicycle became more than a source of transportation for me. The bicycle actually began to truly shape the way I saw the world.

In efforts to restart the lives of those devastated by the crushing waves of the 2004 Indian Ocean tsunami, my husband, F. K. Day, and I founded World Bicycle Relief (WBR). WBR works to provide access to independence and livelihood through the power of bicycles. During our work in Sri Lanka in 2005-2006, we put more than 24,000 new bicycles into the hands of those rebuilding their lives. Since 2006, we have moved into Africa where we currently work in Zambia, Zimbabwe, and Kenya addressing oppressive poverty and the AIDS pandemic by mobilizing volunteer caregivers, students, and entrepreneurs with bicycles.

As WBR's resident photographer I am privileged to see firsthand the impact bicycles have on the lives of our recipients. *Wheels of Change* is a book about history, but today bicycles still empower women. I have met many in Zambia who tell me the bicycle has changed their lives, saved lives, gotten the sick to clinics, brought goods to market and made day-to-day things a whole lot better. Mary Lewanika, a student living in rural Zambia, is having a profound experience in being empowered to steer her own course. At 17, in 2009, Lewanika was the very first student to receive a World Bicycle Relief bike. That day she said she felt safer

Mary Lewanika

already on the long, sometimes dangerous path to and from school. This is particularly important for Lewanika, as she wants to stay in school and graduate from college to become a doctor. After completing another year of school, Lewanika said in 2010, "It is unlikely I would have made it to the eighth grade if I didn't have a bicycle."

Leah Missbach Day

It is a challenge for many African girl students to remain in school. A myriad of obstacles often stand in their way. They have so many chores to do in the morning they often cannot get to school or start their lessons on time. Or, their parents need them to take care of younger siblings while they go work in the fields—a job they would never bestow on their boy children. It used to take Lewanika an hour to walk to and from school. Now her biking commute is 20 minutes. Lewanika is able to get her chores done, make it to school on time, and feel refreshed enough to pay attention in class.

Studies continue to prove that if a girl stays in school she will strengthen her family, community, and nation. A long list of benefits of educating a girl in a developing country compiled by the World Health Organization includes later marriages, smaller families, better hygiene, greatly increased likelihood that further children will receive education, and my favorite—greater confidence. A bicycle is a simple, sustainable tool that eases long travel distances and encourages girls to stay in school.

Freedom comes in many forms. For Mary Lewanika, a bicycle provides freedom from social oppression. A bicycle can cultivate independence. In *Wheels of Change*, Sue Macy quotes Ellen B. Parkhurst in Washington's *Evening Times,* "A girl who rides a wheel is lifted out of herself and her surroundings." That was true in 1896, and incredibly, it remains true in places around the world today.

You see? The bicycle really can change the way you see the world.

Leah Missbach Day
World Bicycle Relief

The author at age four, a few years before her candy-store adventures.

Introduction

When I was a kid, I took great pleasure in jumping on my bike and riding to the corner candy store about half a mile away. Although I had no knowledge of the part the bicycle had played as a vehicle of change for turn-of-the-20th-century women, I was acutely aware that it allowed this 1960s girl a unique measure of independence. On my bike, I could break free of the bonds that held me in my neighborhood to go buy Necco Wafers and candy necklaces and Atomic FireBalls. If I felt particularly adventurous, I could even ride a bit farther for a fresh ice-cream cone at Applegate Farm.

That said, it's hard to grasp the full extent of the bicycle's impact on Americans in the late 19th century—particularly female Americans. Imagine a population imprisoned by their very clothing; the stiff corsets, heavy skirts, and voluminous petticoats that made it difficult to take a deep breath, let alone exercise. Add to that the laws and social conventions that cemented a man's

"To men, the bicycle in the beginning was merely a new toy, another machine added to the long list of devices they knew in their work and play.

To women, it was a steed upon which they rode into a new world."

"WOMAN AND THE WHEEL," *Munsey's Magazine*, May 1896

place as head of the household and holder of the purse strings. How suffocated women must have felt. And how liberated they must have been as they pedaled their wheels toward new horizons.

Wheels of Change looks at how the bicycle took America by storm in the 1880s and '90s, and especially at the ways in which it changed women's lives. It also explores the bicycle culture of the era with short features, appearing after each chapter, that highlight the impact of the two-wheeler on everyday life. You'll meet celebrity cyclists of the day, learn cycling slang, read about cycling songs and magazines, and see bicycles used in advertisements for everything from carpets to candy to baking flour.

Writing this book helped satisfy my curiosity about a topic I first encountered in the early 1990s. While working on *Winning Ways*, my social history of American women in sports, I came across an item about Jane Yatman and Jane Lindsay, who took turns holding long-distance cycling records over and over again in 1899. I also read the reflections of Frances Willard, president of the Woman's Christian Temperance Union, on how and why she learned to ride a bicycle at age 53. Both suggested that there was a story to be told about women and bicycles at the turn of the century. It proved to be a colorful story indeed. I hope you enjoy the ride.

INVENTING the BI

Notice anything unusual about the woman's highwheel bicycle? It's a sidesaddle model, built with both pedals on the same side of the tires to make it easier for women to get on and off and to ride wearing long skirts.

> *The history of the bicycle is modern. The study of its evolution shows the development of a great industry, constantly introducing and applying improvements.*

MARIA E. WARD · *Bicycling for Ladies*, 1896

cycle

SOMETIME BETWEEN MAY AND

November, 1876, Colonel Albert Augustus Pope took a trip that changed American life forever. It didn't happen overnight. But this one sojourn, to Philadelphia, Pennsylvania, from Pope's home near Boston, Massachusetts, was the first step in a chain of events that ultimately led to the rise of the bicycle, the fall of the horse, the paving of America's roadways, the dawn of modern advertising, and the development of the automobile. Equally important, it helped American women gain increased independence, better health, freedom from restrictive clothing, and eventually, the right to vote.

It started innocently enough. Pope, 33, traveled to the City of Brotherly Love to attend the Centennial Exhibition, a celebration commemorating the signing of the Declaration of Independence 100 years before. On the fairgrounds along the Schuylkill River, Pope and close to 10 million others visited exhibits that showcased the latest developments in science and industry, everything from Alexander Graham Bell's telephone to Heinz Ketchup. If they cared to, they could even pay 50 cents to climb up the 32-foot raised right arm and torch of the Statue of Liberty, which had arrived from France the previous year. The money would be used to help assemble the statue and build its pedestal at its permanent home in New York Harbor.

What interested Pope, however, was a display in one of the English buildings, where two manufacturers from Great Britain presented the latest bicycles. Pope was tantalized by these bicycles, called high wheelers, which had huge wheels in the front and tiny ones in the back. A Civil War veteran and entrepreneur, he wondered about the machine's possibilities as both a business venture and a means of transportation. If only it didn't seem so impossible to ride. Pope dismissed the idea of investing in this new vehicle until he encountered another one the following spring, during a jaunt on a horse near his Massachusetts home. All at once, a man on a high wheeler sped by him. When Pope's horse couldn't catch the cyclist, even

In England, high wheelers were called penny farthings because the relationship of the front wheel to the back wheel resembled that of the large British penny coin to the smaller farthing (quarter penny) coin.

After pioneering the development of the bicycle in the United States, Albert Pope became one of the first American manufacturers to produce electric automobiles.

at a gallop, the businessman suddenly saw the potential of traveling on two wheels.

Pope learned to ride a high wheeler himself that summer and then imported eight of them from England. He opened a riding school at the headquarters of his Pope Manufacturing Company, which produced supplies used in making shoes. He also convinced the president of a sewing machine company in Hartford, Connecticut, to analyze one of his bicycles and make 50 more in his factory. Before long, Pope converted his own business to focus solely on bicycles and took a trip to England to study the industry there. Upon his return, he found one big obstacle. Through the years, a number of individuals had taken out patents that gave them exclusive rights to specific devices and improvements they had invented for the bicycle. If Pope wanted to use these, he would have to pay the patent holders royalties totaling $15 or more for each bicycle he produced. Instead, Pope bought the patents from the inventors outright. That gave him the unrestricted use of all their innovations.

BY THE TIME POPE ENTERED THE BICYCLE
business, people had been imagining and tinkering with various human-powered vehicles for more than 200 years. One of the first references to a two-wheeled device was an image in a stained-glass window created in 1642 at St. Giles Church in Stoke Poges, Buckinghamshire, England. But it wasn't until 1817 that Baron Karl von Drais of Germany built a *laufmaschine* (running machine) that included some of the features that would carry through to the modern bicycle. An early edition of the *Encyclopædia Britannica* described Drais's vehicle as "at the best an awkward affair, composed of a couple of heavy wooden wheels of equal diameter, one behind the other, and joined together by a longitudinal wooden bar on which the rider's seat was fixed, the mode of propulsion being the pushing [of] the feet against the ground." Riders steered the

PLAYER'S CIGARETTES

LADY'S PEDESTRIAN HOBBY-HORSE

Starting in 1893, John Player & Sons of Great Britain issued collectible cards on a number of topics in its packages of cigarettes. This card is from a series on bicycle history issued in 1939.

machine using a handle that moved the front wheel. Drais reported that a person could travel eight to nine miles per hour on his invention on dry, level ground and faster downhill.

Drais's machine became known as a *draisine*, but also was

St. Giles Church, with a bicycle-like image in one of its stained-glass windows, also has a second claim to fame. Many believe that poet Thomas Gray wrote his "Elegy Written in a Country Churchyard" in the church's graveyard.

called a velocipede, from the Latin words meaning "swift of foot." This vehicle was quickly copied and improved upon by others, including Englishman Denis Johnson, who made the seat adjustable and added an armrest between the seat and the steering handle. Johnson added further alterations in a version for women, dropping the horizontal bar that linked the wheels to make room for their skirts. Johnson's machines, referred to as dandy horses, or more commonly, hobbyhorses, were briefly popular among the wealthier classes in England and parts of the United States. But with no brakes and with their main power coming from the rider's feet running along the ground, these wooden "horses" had their limitations.

Inventors began to explore the idea of attaching cranks or pedals to the velocipede's wheels as early as the 1820s. Although a few made successful models for personal use, no one developed a prototype that gained widespread acceptance until the 1860s. Some attribute the breakthrough to Ernest Michaux, a French carriage maker, though others credit Pierre Lallement, who worked for him. At any rate, the new velocipede was propelled by pedals and cranks attached directly to the axel of the front wheel, which was slightly larger than the wheel behind it. Forward progress could be stopped or slowed by pedaling

Samuel Webb Thomas designed this variation of the boneshaker for women. Like the high wheeler on page 10, it was meant to be ridden sidesaddle and has both pedals on the left side.

backward. However, with iron tires and only an ineffective steel spring under the seat to absorb bumps in the road, this velocipede was a challenge to ride. It quickly earned the nickname "boneshaker." In 1865, Lallement brought his boneshaker to Connecticut, where he filed a description of it with the federal government and received a patent. While the boneshaker enjoyed a flash of popularity in the United States and Europe, its weight—it could be as heavy as 150 pounds—and other design flaws hastened its demise.

as a new decade began, inventors focused on fine-tuning the two-wheeler in four main areas: weight, speed, performance, and comfort. In 1870, the British firm of Starley and Company patented the Ariel, which, quite literally, was the shape of things to come. Its front wheel was about 48 inches high and dramatically larger than its rear wheel. Since each revolution of the pedals translated to one revolution of the front wheel, the rider could cover more ground with less effort than on a boneshaker. Meanwhile, the small rear wheel kept down the weight of the machine. Soon there were other innovations. Solid rubber tires and pedals replaced metal ones. Frames were made of steel instead of iron or wood. Seat springs were improved and brakes were added. The weight was reduced to 50 and then 40 pounds. Each of these changes distanced the velocipede from its origins as a machine for the "swift of foot" until finally, a new term became popular for the two-wheeled wonder: bicycle. The high wheeler later came to be known as an ordinary, to distinguish it from other bicycles.

In 1878, Albert Pope was ready to launch the American bicycle industry with his own Columbia brand of high wheelers. But building bicycles was only half the battle. Pope knew that he also had to build a market by raising

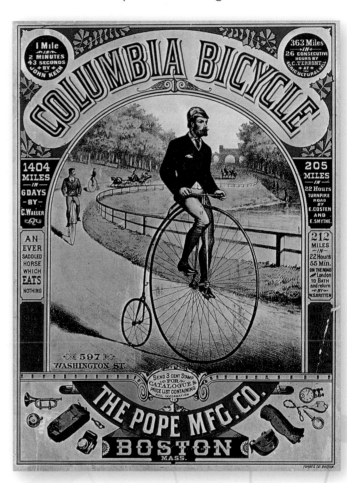

Albert Pope's use of posters and magazine ads to sell his Columbia bicycles helped to popularize these marketing techniques.

the excitement level of the American people for his product. He accomplished this on several fronts, starting with the written word. Pope imported the best cycling articles and pamphlets from England and distributed them to potential customers. He encouraged American author Charles E. Pratt to write *The American Bicycler*, a handbook for cyclists, and gave away thousands of copies after it was published in 1879. He helped to underwrite a monthly magazine, *The Wheelman* (later called *Outing*), and gave prizes to doctors who wrote the most effective articles linking bicycle riding to good health.

While he nurtured the popularity of the bicycle through the press, Pope also supported legal and political efforts to establish cycling as a legitimate endeavor. That included going to court in cities where riding was outlawed on streets or in parks based on claims that cycles frightened horses. In New York City, for example, three cyclists were arrested in 1881 for defying an ordinance against riding in Central Park. This was a test case, and Pope was more than willing to finance the defendants' legal battle. Months of testimony ensued, starting with witness Samuel G. Hough, who described what happened when a cyclist crashed into his horse-drawn buggy. The crash caused his horses to run away, Hough said, flipping over the buggy and killing one of the animals. "I consider the bicycle to be the most dangerous thing to life and property ever invented," exclaimed Hough, who suffered a broken arm and finger in the accident. "The gentlest of horses are afraid of it." In the end, the judge upheld the right of New York's parks commissioners to ban bicycles and fined the cyclists five dollars each.

Pope was not alone in his determination to fight for the rights of American cyclists. In the spring of 1880, he had joined author Charles Pratt and others in forming the League of American Wheelmen ("the L.A.W."), an organization that pledged to "promote the general interests of bicycling, to ascertain, defend, and protect the rights of wheelmen, and to

inventive women

Hundreds of creative individuals received U.S. patents for bicycle-related inventions in the late 1880s and 1890s. Among them were a handful of women. Here are a few, along with descriptions of their inventions from the original documents granting their patents.

Kate Parke, Chicago, Illinois: Bicycle Lock, 1890 "My present invention has, primarily, for its object to provide [an] improved lock mechanism whereby bicycles may be locked to prevent them from being used without the owner's consent or to prevent them from being stolen."

Alice A. Bennitt, Elgin, Illinois: Bicycle-Canopy, 1896 "My object is to provide a canopy and supports that may be readily attached to a bicycle or detached and folded compactly for storage when not in use, simple in design and cheaply manufactured."

Mary F. Henderson, District of Columbia: Bicycle-Saddle, 1896, and Bicycle-Saddle, 1897 (two patents) "The object of the present invention is to provide a cushioned seat supported by a saddle-frame which will secure comfort and safety to the rider." (1897)

Sarah C. Clagett, Prince Georges County, Maryland: Bicycle-Skirt Fastener, 1897 "The object of my invention is to afford a cheap, simple, and effective means for holding down the skirt of a lady's dress while riding the bicycle."

Agness Amess and Maude A. Powlison, Perth, North Dakota: Bicycle Stand and Lock, 1899 "The invention has for its object to construct a combination stand and lock for bicycles and like vehicles which will be simple in its construction, strong, durable, effectual in its operation, and comparatively inexpensive to manufacture."

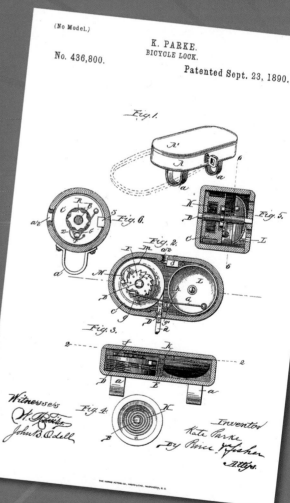

Diagrams from Kate Parke's patent application, 1890

aLice austen

In 1896, when Maria E. "Violet" Ward published her how-to book, *Bicycling for Ladies*, she included 34 photographs showing women how to mount, ride, and repair their wheels. Ward's photographer was Alice Austen, a childhood friend from Staten Island, New York, and like herself, a talented athlete. Austen also was one of the earliest and most prolific female photographers, taking upward of 8,000 photographs of immigrants, laborers, socialites, nature scenes, and historic events. Later in life, she was called the "female Mathew Brady," a reference to the pioneering Civil War photographer.

Austen received her first camera from her uncle in 1877, when she was 11 years old. Another uncle, a chemistry professor, taught her how to use photographic chemicals in a darkroom. A dedicated cyclist, Austen often rode to assignments in New York on her bicycle, loaded down with 50 pounds of camera equipment. She stopped taking pictures after she lost much of her money in the stock market crash of 1929; she could no longer afford to buy film. Austen was rediscovered late in life, when some of her photographs were exhibited and published. She died in 1952 at age 86.

Besides her work in the United States, Austen took a total of 22 trips abroad to photograph scenes in France, England, and Germany.

encourage and facilitate touring." The L.A.W. was a powerful lobby group that did its best to overturn bans. But its influence didn't end there. The group organized bicycle races, developed maps for touring cyclists, endorsed bicycle-friendly restaurants and hotels, and perhaps most critically, launched a movement intent on establishing bicycle paths and improving the nation's roads.

GOOD ROADS WERE ESSENTIAL TO THE SUCCESS

of the bicycle. While the prospect of a ride in the country had romantic appeal to many cyclists, the roads that awaited them were rocky and uneven, blowing up clouds of dust in dry weather and turning into muddy pits in the rain. City streets might be paved, but they still presented all sorts of hazards, from uneven cobblestones and raised trolley tracks to ruts made by horses, buggies, and peddlers' carts. Since riders on ordinaries sat high above

the center of gravity of their cycles, any bump or rut could make them lose their balance and "take a header" (plunge headfirst) over the front wheel. On its members' behalf, the L.A.W. campaigned for separate bicycle paths in cities and pointed out to farmers that better rural roads would save their horses from injury. The smooth surfaces, claimed the organization, would also allow farmers

As the demand for bicycles grew in the 1890s, so did the demand for accessories—such as bells, locks, and lamps—and repairs. This photograph shows the Joseph H. Ferodowill bicycle repair shop in St. Paul, Minnesota, in 1899.

21

to use fewer horses to move their goods to market, resulting in an annual saving of $700 million on horse feed alone. Before long, farmers stood squarely with the L.A.W. in the campaign for better roads. For their trouble, they saw the farmland along newly paved roads double in value.

Proponents of road improvements made little progress in the 1880s, largely because throughout most of the decade, there were fewer than 50,000 cyclists in the entire United States.

Brooklyn Eagle (Brooklyn, New York)

MARCH 16, 1869

Velocipede Talk

WITTY'S FEMALE SCHOOL — In a short time — as soon as arrangements are completed, Mr. H. B. Witty will open a ladies' velocipede riding school. The room will be in his building in Nevins street, where he has a fine large room, to which there will be an entrance entirely distinct from the other entrance. Miss Carrie Moore, the skater and who is also a fine rider of the velocipede, will have charge of the room and will act as instructress. Garments of the Bloomer pattern, will be kept on hand for those who wish to ride. No gentlemen will be admitted to the room, so that sensitive and bashful ladies need not be afraid of intrusion. It is to be hoped that the ladies will patronize the bicycles, for it will prove to be a great benefit to them in the way of exercise.

That changed dramatically in 1887 with the American debut of the latest innovation from England, the "safety." As the name implies, this new bicycle, with two wheels of equal or almost equal size, was designed to eliminate the danger riders faced on high wheelers. Besides having a lower center of gravity, the safety's seat, or saddle, was toward the rear of the bike, making headers less likely. The new bicycle also had pedals attached to a chain-and-sprocket mechanism that added speed and efficiency. And starting in 1889, manufacturers offered the biggest improvement yet: cushiony pneumatic tires, which were rubber on the outside but filled with compressed air.

The sum total of all these developments was a machine that was accessible to anyone with the confidence and willpower to learn to ride and the wherewithal to buy, rent, or borrow a bike. In the United States during the 1890s, that was just about everyone.

remember the Ladies

Before the safety was invented, most bicycles were designed with men in mind. The long, full dresses that women wore made riding boneshakers difficult and ordinaries pretty near impossible. But bicycle makers realized there was money to be made in offering women a cycling option, and they came up with some interesting, if not always practical, designs.

Sidesaddle: Women in skirts traditionally rode horses sidesaddle, with both legs on the same side of the animal. So some manufacturers gave sidesaddle bicycles a try. In 1870, a sidesaddle boneshaker had two pedals on the left-hand side of the bike. Four years later, James Starley, of Ariel fame, developed a sidesaddle ordinary that was driven by a lever on the left side. Neither solution proved successful.

Tricycles: The first three-wheel cycles debuted in the days of the draisine. They involved three riders, usually male, each working a hand crank to drive the vehicle. But when British companies started offering single-seat, pedal-driven tricycles in the late 1870s, they found a market in wealthy women, doctors visiting patients, and delivery people, who used the machine's storage compartment to carry their wares. The machine earned the royal stamp of approval after Queen Victoria of England ordered two. In 1877, James Starley introduced a two-seat tricycle called the Salvo Sociable that became popular with couples.

Image from the Sociable Tricycle Player's card

Tandem Bicycles: On these "bicycles built for two," riders sat one behind the other and both pedaled to drive the vehicle. The first tandem bicycle was available in England in 1888, and within a decade, most American manufacturers were offering at least one model. While some racers competed on tandems, these cycles also attracted those intent on romance.

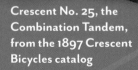

Crescent No. 25, the Combination Tandem, from the 1897 Crescent Bicycles catalog

Drop Frames: In 1888, Mrs. W. E. Smith of Washington, D.C., looked over her husband's new safety bicycle and decided she wanted one, too. But the high bar between the seat and handlebars—part of the sturdy diamond-shaped core of the machine—got in the way of her skirts. Her husband tinkered with the bicycle and invented the drop frame, with the center bar swooping down low to make room for skirts and dresses. It soon became the standard for women's safeties everywhere.

New York Times (New York, New York)

SEPTEMBER 24, 1892

World's Records for One Mile by Various Methods of Progression.

Time for One Mile	Method of Progression	Names of Record Holders	Place Where Made	Date
0:39⅘	Railway train	Phil. & Reading R.R.	New York Division	Aug. 27, 1891
1:10	Yacht (ice)	*Dreadnought*	Red Bank, N.J.	Jan. 26, 1884
1:35½	Horse (running)	Salvator	Monmouth Park, N.J.	Aug. 28, 1890
2:05¼	Horse (trotting)	Nancy Hanks	Independence, Iowa	Aug. 31, 1892
2:06⅘	Safety bicycle	A. A. Zimmerman	Springfield, Mass.	Sept. 9, 1892
2:12⅗	Skating (ice, with wind)	T. Donoghue	Newburgh, N.Y.	Feb. 1, 1887
2:14⅘	Tandem bicycle	G. Banker & C. Hess	Springfield, Mass.	Sept. 8, 1892
2:25⅗	Ordinary bicycle	W. W. Windle	Peoria, Ill.	Sept. 15, 1890
2:28⅖	Single tricycle	Cassignard	Courbevoie Track, France	Oct. 18, 1891
2:31⅖	Tandem tricycle	P. W. S. Beduin and B. W. Crump	Herne Hill, London, Eng.	1891
2:50⅖	Skating (roller)	F. Delmont	Olympia, London, Eng.	Aug. 27, 1890
2:55⅖	Skating (ice, 5-lap track)	O. Grunden	Stockholm, Sweden	Feb. 23, 1890
4:12¾	Running	W. G. George	Lillie Bridge, London, Eng.	Aug. 23, 1886
5:39⅗	Snowshoes (running)	J. F. Scholes	Montreal, Canada	Feb. 22, 1871
5:40	Rowing (single sculls)	J. Laing	Lachine, Canada	Aug. 19, 1882
6:23	Walking	W. Perkins	Lillie Bridge, London, Eng.	June 1, 1874
9:29	Canoe (paddling)	A. F. McKendrick	Jessup's Neck	Aug. 20, 1890
28:19¾	Swimming	J. J. Collier	Hollingsworth Lake, Eng.	Aug. 23, 1884

In June 1894, the first dedicated bicycle path in the United States opened in Brooklyn, New York. Part of Ocean Parkway, a roadway stretching from Prospect Park to Coney Island, the path had to be widened several times to accommodate heavy bicycle traffic.

In less than a decade, the growing bicycle craze created one of the largest industries in the country. In 1885, the heyday of the ordinary, there were only six cycle manufacturers in the United States, with a total annual output of 11,000 bicycles. Five years later, with the safety now available, there were 17 manufacturers, and they produced 40,000 bicycles. In 1895, the *New York Times* reported the existence of 126 manufacturers with an expected annual output of "nearly half a million machines in this country alone." And annual production reached one million bicycles in 1896. What's more, a network of bicycle repair shops sprouted up overnight, as did businesses that made related products, including tires, lamps, whistles, locks, shoes, and clothing. According to one estimate, by May 1896, Americans had spent $300 million on bicycles (at $50 to $125 or more per machine) and $200 million on related products. But the impact of America's sudden, intense love affair with the bicycle went far beyond the world of business and industry, and not everyone thought it was positive. In fact, at least one social commentator believed American women were riding the wheel straight to hell.

ceLebRITY
cycLists

Cycling was all the rage in the late 1800s, so it's not surprising that some of the more well-known women in the United States—and the world—regularly took their wheels for a spin.

Riding Toward Equality—One of the first female lawyers in the United States, Belva Lockwood, left, achieved an even bigger "first" in 1884 when she became the first woman ever to appear on the official ballot as a candidate for U.S. President. By that time, this Equal Rights Party candidate also had gained attention for her practice of riding an English tricycle, like the one shown at left, to work in Washington, D.C. After the Washington Post ran an article about Lockwood and her "three-footed nag," she responded with a poem describing herself as

A simple home woman, who only had thought

To lighten the labors her business had wrought.

And make a machine serve the purpose of feet.

And at the same time keep her dress from the street.

AKAUER BR

NEW YORK

Dressing the Part—Frances Benjamin Johnston, right, might have raised a few eyebrows when she donned a man's suit and a fake mustache for this self-portrait in the late 1800s. But the groundbreaking photographer was used to operating in a man's world. Besides gaining fame for her portraits of the important figures of her era, she served as the official White House photographer under five presidents: Benjamin Harrison, Grover Cleveland, William McKinley, Theodore Roosevelt, and William Howard Taft.

The Wright Stuff—Katharine Wright, shown on the title page, came by her interest in the bicycle honestly. Her older brothers, Orville and Wilbur Wright, opened a bicycle sales and repair shop in 1892 and even designed their own bicycle model before turning their interest to airplanes. Wright later would play an important part in her brothers' efforts to develop and market the plane they invented in 1903. In the photo, Wright, second from right, is about to leave on a bicycle outing with friends at Oberlin College in 1898.

Annie Get Your Wheel—In 1892, sharpshooter Annie Oakley, left, gave an interview to Britain's *The Cycle Record* about her new bicycle. "I am delighted with my wheel," she said. "I am equally as fond of it as my horse." Oakley said she intended to make her bicycle part of her shooting act in Buffalo Bill's Wild West show. Soon she taught herself to ride without holding the handlebars while successfully shooting at glass balls that an assistant threw in the air. In this photo, Oakley is seen in 1893, relaxing outside her living quarters at the World's Columbian Exposition in Chicago, Illinois, with her shotguns and bicycle close at hand.

A Nobel Pursuit—Marie Curie and her husband, Pierre, left, celebrated their marriage in 1895 with a honeymoon bicycle trip. The couple, avid cyclists, went on to win the 1903 Nobel Prize in Physics for their research on radioactivity. Marie would also win the 1911 Nobel Prize in chemistry for discovering the elements radium and polonium. She was the first woman ever awarded a Nobel Prize, and the first person to win or share two of these honors.

Background: Detail of a woman on a tricycle from an ad for Krakauer Pianos

> *Many a girl has come to her ruin through a spin on a country road.*
>
> CHARLOTTE SMITH · *Brooklyn Eagle*, August 20, 1896

"THE DEVIL'S AD

IT WAS JUNE 29, 1896, AND CHARLOTTE Smith was beside herself with concern for the young women of the United States. Smith, the 55-year-old daughter of Irish immigrants, had spent the last decade and a half fighting for the rights of female workers. But now all of her worries about their health and well-being were focused on one wildly popular mechanical object: the bicycle.

"Bicycling by young women has helped to swell the ranks of reckless girls who finally drift into the standing army of outcast women of the United States," wrote Smith in a resolution issued by her group, the Women's Rescue League. "The bicycle is the devil's advance agent morally and physically in thousands of instances." Smith's resolution called for "all true women and clergymen" to join with her in

vance agent"

Charlotte Smith was afraid that any innocent bicycle ride could turn into a romantic interlude like the one shown on this postcard from 1905. In the full image, the gentleman's bicycle is seen cast aside on the ground to his right.

denouncing the bicycle craze among women as "indecent and vulgar." She set her sights on New York City as the laboratory for her reform efforts, opening a branch of her Washington-based organization there with the goal of ultimately limiting the use of the bicycle by women. Smith blamed the bicycle for the downfall of women's health, morals, and religious devotion. Her accusations brought a swift and impassioned response. The Reverend Dr. A. Stewart Walsh, a respected clergyman in New York City and a cyclist himself, wrote a letter to the editor of the *Brooklyn Eagle* declaring, "I have associated with thousands of riders . . . and I have not seen among them . . . anything that could begin to approach the outrageous and scandalous indecency of the resolutions of the alleged rescue league." Ellen B. Parkhurst, wife of another New York minister, celebrated the advantages of bicycle riding in Washington's *Evening Times*. "Of course I do not believe that bicycling is immoral,"

A couple on a tandem, or bicycle built for two, enjoys a ride in the park in 1899.

MISS FLY

2859

COPYRIGHT, 1897, BY AMERICAN LITHOGRAPHIC CO., REG. IN U.S. PATENT OFFICE.

LITHO. WITSCH & SCHMITT, N.Y.

Although the popularity of the bicycle caused people to buy and smoke fewer cigars, female cyclists frequently graced the labels of cigar boxes, such as the one shown here.

she said. "A girl who rides a wheel is lifted out of herself and her surroundings. She is made to breathe purer air, see fresher and more beautiful scenes, and get an amount of exercise she would not otherwise get. All this is highly beneficial."

In fact, the impact of the bicycle on the health and welfare of its riders was the subject of a great deal of discussion in the 1890s. At first, the popularity of the safety drew mostly praise as its use seemed to usher in a new era of robust living. Medical literature linked cycling to cures for everything from asthma and diabetes to heart disease and varicose veins, while one study credited the decreasing death rate from consumption (tuberculosis) among women in Massachusetts to their increasing use of the bicycle. Cigar sales took a hit—one industry estimate suggested people were buying as many as one million fewer cigars *per day*—because cyclists were too

CHARLOTTE SMITH

In her obituary on December 4, 1917, the *Boston Globe* called Charlotte Smith "one of Boston's most picturesque personalities." It was, most decidedly, an understatement. This outspoken feminist spent a lifetime fighting to secure and safeguard rights for women, sometimes by taking unusual, unpopular stands. Her opposition to the bicycle on the grounds that "it has a tendency to lure young girls into paths that lead directly to sin" drew much criticism. It even earned Smith an entry in the satirical *Devil's Dictionary*, where author Ambrose Bierce included a verse about Charlotte to help define the term "smithereen."

Beyond her bicycle campaign, Smith made a national impact as a crusader and a lobbyist. She founded the Women's National Industrial League, an all-female union for federal clerks, and started and edited two periodicals focusing on women, the *Working Woman* and the *Woman Inventor*. Her lobbying efforts led the U.S. Patent Office to issue its first-ever list of female patent holders in 1888. Moving from Washington, D.C., to Boston in 1892, she opened a lodging house for working girls and later organized the Women's Board of Trade to promote collaboration among businesswomen. All the while, Smith carried on a quirkier, more personal effort to convince men to treat women with respect. Whenever she saw a man annoying a young woman, she bashed him over the head with her umbrella. Smith estimated that she destroyed at least 5,000 umbrellas in the process.

Charlotte Smith's weapon of choice

busy exercising to indulge in the smoking habit. And in Chicago, bicycling evidently caused a drop in the use of the painkiller morphine. "The morphine takers have discovered that a long spin in the fresh air on a cycle induces sweet sleep better than their favorite drug," reported the *British Medical Journal* in November 1895.

as enthusiasts spent more and more

time on their bicycles, however, doctors, clergy members, and social commentators started to question this love affair with the wheel. In 1896, the *Journal of the American Medical Association* published a cautionary article by Dr. William C. Krauss of Buffalo, New York, that reported the curious case of a 37-year-old man with "acute dilation of the heart." It seems the patient, James H.C., regularly cycled the half mile to and from his job on the railroad, but on one occasion, he took a four-mile, 25-minute ride with his friends that left him severely distressed. At the end of it, his heart was pounding, he had a severe pain on the left side of his chest, and he was completely out of breath. James heeded his friends' advice and rode home immediately, covering the distance a bit more slowly. But his symptoms worsened overnight, and his heart was still racing at 130 beats per minute when Krauss saw him two months later. The doctor's diagnosis was short and to the point: "over-bicycling." He explained, "The distance covered and the time would be insignificant to a trained wheelman, but to one not accustomed to long rides it was quite an undertaking and was fraught with serious consequences."

By the time Krauss published his case study, other physicians had begun chronicling a wide variety of medical ills allegedly related to the bicycle. Dr. Benjamin Ward Richardson of Great Britain, a big fan of the wheel, nevertheless summarized its pitfalls in his 1895 article "What To Avoid in Cycling." Among those pitfalls were several dangers that resulted from "teaching the practice to subjects who are too young." Richardson believed serious riding should not be done by males or females until the skeleton was completely matured, which he said happened around age 21. "The spinal column is particularly apt to be injured by too early riding," he wrote, because cyclists tended to bend their bodies forward as they rode. "The spine more or less permanently assumes the bent position." He went on to warn that the hearts, muscles, and nervous systems of riders also

Sporting Life (Philadelphia, Pennsylvania)

OCTOBER 14, 1893

Mrs. Burrows and Her Bicycle

BINGHAMTON, NY., OCT. 9 — The High Street Methodist Church is now in a turmoil over the propriety of women riding bicycles. The trouble began when Mrs. Burrows, a widow, purchased a bicycle. She is an active worker in the church.

At a prayer-meeting the other night Samuel Stanley arose and denounced the act of bicycle-riding as unladylike, unchristian and a disgrace to the church. The deacon edified the audience by an attempted illustration of a woman riding a bicycle. The pastor, Rev. John Bradshaw, took sides against the bicyclists.

Mrs. Burrows' friends threaten to carry the question before the next conference. The Young Women's Christian Association has established a wheel club in open defiance of those who disapprove of bicycles.

A child rides a tricycle in the park near the New York City church of Dr. Parkhurst, whose wife Ellen was a great supporter of cycling for women.

might be adversely
affected if they started
cycling too early.

Richardson's British colleagues devoted much attention to health-related issues arising from the bicycle. In 1896, the *British Medical Journal* ran a 10-part series titled "A Report on Cycling in Health and Disease," which was prepared by E. B. Turner, vice president of England's National Cyclists' Union. Installments focused on such subjects as "The Limits of Age for Cycling," "Cycling Accidents," and "Cycling for Women." Regarding women, Turner declared, "With hardly any exception there is a consensus of opinion that the exercise of wheeling, properly regulated and indulged in at proper times and seasons, is of great benefit to all sound women and girls." However, Turner warned that women should not indulge in racing. "It must be distinctly understood that anything in the way of racing or speed competition on cycles must be injurious to any woman," he wrote, "and should never be allowed." He also cautioned women not to cycle during their menstrual periods, while they were pregnant, or for three months after giving birth.

In the morally conservative 1890s, commentators on women and the bicycle often touched on issues related to sex and reproduction. Not too long before, doctors and others had argued that women who took part in any type of physical fitness activity, other than dance, would jeopardize their ability to have children. This thinking slowly changed, thanks in large part to women's schools and colleges that turned out healthy students fit for motherhood despite a steady diet of calisthenics, or light gymnastic exercises, as well as horseback riding, swimming, boating, and ice skating. Still, some feared women would injure their pelvic organs through the repeated motion of the limbs that was necessary to pedal a bicycle. Others worried that the shape of the bicycle seat, or saddle, could damage or over-stimulate the pelvis. One solution was the raising of the handlebars of a woman's bicycle, which required her to sit straight up and toward the back of the saddle. Another was the development of special women's seats, which had a smaller than usual peak in front or no peak at all.

aLthough they raReLy

said it, some of those who focused on the effects of cycling on women's sexual and reproductive health had a greater concern. They worried that the bicycle might permanently change women's role in society by fostering their independence. At the time, the social lives of many young women were strictly supervised, but cycling allowed these women to escape their parents' watchful eyes. "Parents who will not allow their daughters to accompany young men to the theatre without chaperonage allow them to go bicycle-riding alone with young men," newspaperman Joseph Bishop wrote in an assessment of the impact of the bicycle in 1896. This was one of the matters that motivated Charlotte Smith to declare that the bicycle had brought about "the alarming increase of immorality among young women in the United States" because of the "evil associations and opportunities" it made possible.

It's surprising, then, that the members of the clergy on whom Smith was depending to rail against female cyclists didn't always agree with her. Indeed, the issue for most clergy members was not whether women

Four cyclists stop for a photograph on the Alameda Avenue bridge in Denver, Colorado, circa 1905. Before the bicycle, young people often had adult supervision when they socialized.

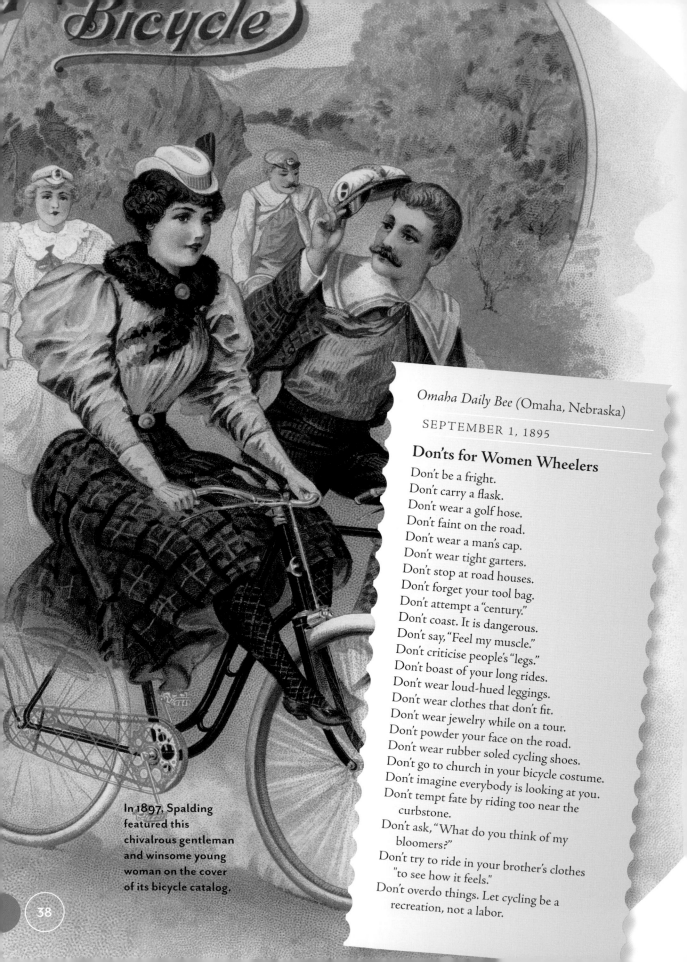

Bicycle

In 1897, Spalding featured this chivalrous gentleman and winsome young woman on the cover of its bicycle catalog.

Omaha Daily Bee (Omaha, Nebraska)

SEPTEMBER 1, 1895

Don'ts for Women Wheelers

Don't be a fright.

Don't carry a flask.

Don't wear a golf hose.

Don't faint on the road.

Don't wear a man's cap.

Don't wear tight garters.

Don't stop at road houses.

Don't forget your tool bag.

Don't attempt a "century."

Don't coast. It is dangerous.

Don't say, "Feel my muscle."

Don't criticise people's "legs."

Don't boast of your long rides.

Don't wear loud-hued leggings.

Don't wear clothes that don't fit.

Don't wear jewelry while on a tour.

Don't powder your face on the road.

Don't wear rubber soled cycling shoes.

Don't go to church in your bicycle costume.

Don't imagine everybody is looking at you.

Don't tempt fate by riding too near the curbstone.

Don't ask, "What do you think of my bloomers?"

Don't try to ride in your brother's clothes "to see how it feels."

Don't overdo things. Let cycling be a recreation, not a labor.

should take to the wheel. It was whether, in the era of the six-day work week, cyclists could be persuaded to come to church on Sunday, their only day off. Churches in small cities and towns especially were hit hard by the popularity of the bicycle. "Attendance upon religious services in these places has been helped by the fact that there was little else to do on Sunday," wrote Joseph Bishop. "Now comes the bicycle with a proposal for a social ride into the country on Sunday. . . . It is not in human nature . . . to resist a call like this."

Concerns about inappropriately shaped women's bicycle seats led to the Duplex and other special women's saddles.

To hang on to their flocks, clergy members invited congregants to wear cycling clothes to church and provided space to park their bikes. A few industrious ministers even tried meeting cyclists on their own turf, holding outdoor services on bicycle routes. They had little success.

In the end, Charlotte Smith's attempts to force women off their bicycles failed. The medical experts and religious leaders charged with ensuring women's physical and moral welfare rejected her predictions of doom and damnation as being greatly exaggerated. What's more, women themselves were loath to give up the vehicle that they planned to ride boldly into the new century. Maria E. Ward, author of the 1896 how-to book *Bicycling for Ladies,* characterized the promise of the wheel in glowing terms: "A bright, sunny morning, fresh and cool; good roads and a dry atmosphere; a beautiful country before you, all your own to see and enjoy; a properly adjusted wheel awaiting you, what more delightful than to mount and speed away."

CYCLING SLANG

Not long after Americans embraced the bicycle, new words and phrases started to enter their vocabulary. Here's a look at the "bicycle talk" of the 1890s.

Five "Pet Names" for the Bicycle

These terms, all inspired by the horse, were used affectionately to refer to the bicycle in magazine articles and short stories.

Nickel-clad horse

Silent steed

Steel horse

Steel steed

Willing steed

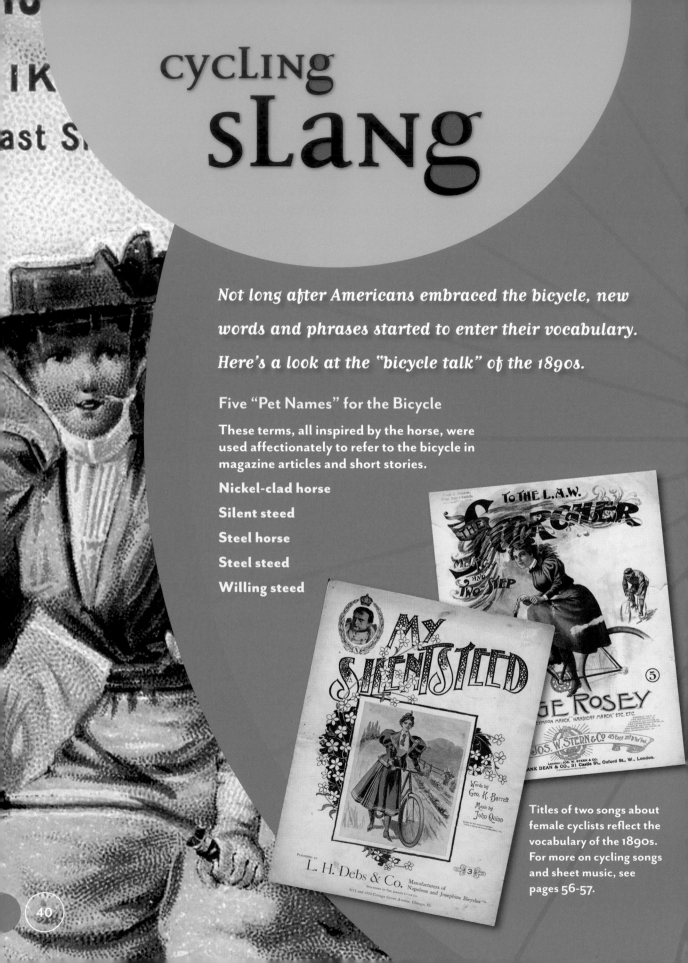

Titles of two songs about female cyclists reflect the vocabulary of the 1890s. For more on cycling songs and sheet music, see pages 56-57.

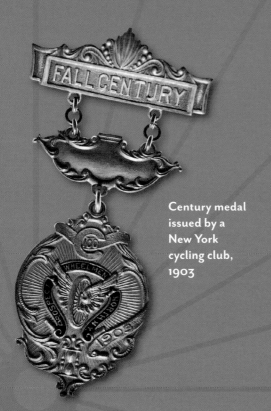

Century medal issued by a New York cycling club, 1903

Medical Terms

During the bicycle craze, doctors attributed a whole host of maladies to people's sudden love affairs with the wheel, including:

Bicycle Eye: Fatigue of the muscles under the eye suffered by cyclists who race with their heads lowered and their backs bent forward and therefore constantly have to raise their eyes to see.

Bicycle Face: The strained look on a cyclist's face, characterized by wide-open eyes, stress lines around the mouth, and a jutting jaw. "The general focus of the features is indicative of extreme attention directed to a spot about two yards ahead of the wheel," explained one newspaper. "This attention arises from a suspicion that there is probably a stone, a bit of glass, an upturned tack, barrel hoop or other dangerous article lying in wait there."

Bicycle Fright: A nervous condition in which a rider who wants desperately to avoid an accident instead makes the accident happen, such as by helplessly steering toward an oncoming vehicle.

Bicycle Hands: A numbness of the hands and fingers that develops from a combination of a tight grip on the handlebars and the vibrations from the bicycle's front wheel.

Bicycle Heart: A heart that is enlarged and/or beating rapidly due to the strain of riding up hills and against the wind; also known as "athlete's heart."

Bicycle Wrists: Sore and swollen wrists resulting from gripping the bicycle's handlebars tightly while riding.

Background: Detail from an advertisement for an Illinois carpet company

General Terms

Century (*noun*): A continuous ride of one hundred miles, as in *I plan to ride a century tomorrow*.

Come a Cropper (*verb*): To be thrown over the front wheel of a bicycle, especially an ordinary. Similar to "take a header." From a British phrase meaning to fail badly.

Corker (*noun*): Something outstanding or first-rate, as in *This ride was a real corker*.

Cracks (*plural noun*): Bicycle racers.

Scorcher (*noun*): A fast or reckless rider, so named because of his or her blazing speed.

fashion

In 1898, actress Alice Hughes poses with a bicycle in a scene from J. M. Barrie's play *A Professor's Love Story*. Six years later, Barrie would write the play for which he is remembered best, *Peter Pan, or The Boy Who Wouldn't Grow Up.*

> "It is an accepted fact that bicycling cannot be properly enjoyed unless the clothing is suitable."

MARIA E. WARD · *Bicycling for Ladies*, 1896

forward

IN THE 1890S, RIDING A BICYCLE in traditional clothing could be hazardous to a woman's health. Witness this all-too-typical account of a female cyclist whose adventure came to an abrupt end: "The wind was behind me, the road good, with just the least bit of down-slope, and I was skimming along like a bird, when there was an awful tug at my dress and a cracking sound," recalled the unnamed woman, who was quoted in the journal *Sporting Life* in October 1891. "Before I knew what was the matter I found myself lying in the road with the safety on the top of me. My dress was so tightly wound round the crank bracket that I could not get up until I had got it free." Although the cyclist was only bruised, her dress was ripped all along the waist. "I had to fasten it up as well as I could with pins," she said. "It is quite certain that women run a great deal of risk over their dresses."

Stories like this underlined the need for more appropriate women's cycling clothing. Yet the rocky history of dress reform in the 19th century left many people suspicious of any change in women's fashion, even for the sake of safety. The problem was that what women wore touched on issues of their larger role in society and of what rights they should have.

Since early in the century, women's clothing seemed to be designed more for beauty and style than for comfort and practicality. One undergarment in particular, the corset, made the very act of getting dressed a challenge. This contraption, usually made with steel and whalebone and worn on the upper part of the body, cinched a woman's waist, lifted her chest, and supported her back. It was secured by laces that were pulled tight and tied in the back, the tighter the better to give a woman an "hourglass" figure. Even young girls wore corsets. One contemporary advertisement suggested that

Women's broad skirts and billowy undergarments frequently inspired humorous commentaries, such as this 1860 cartoon.

Wearing a tightly-laced corset could make it difficult for a woman to breathe. It also could displace and damage internal organs including the liver, lungs, and stomach.

a mother have her daughter lie face down and then place her foot on the girl's back to tighten the laces as much as possible.

BY THE 1840S, DRESSES HAD BECOME longer and fuller, with women wearing several layers of petticoats to create a teepee-like effect from the waist down. Taken together, these floor-length petticoats and the dress that covered them could weigh 25 pounds — even more when the unfortunate woman got caught in a rainstorm. Plus they were unsanitary. During a casual stroll, an unsuspecting fashion plate could pick up cigar ends, cigarette butts, discarded food, tiny insects, and animal droppings as her clothing swept the ground.

Driven by a desire for comfort and physical well-being, several groups of women introduced alternative approaches to fashion in the 1850s. Most combined a dress shortened to about four or five inches below the knee with some sort of baggy pantaloons worn underneath. Women's rights advocates Elizabeth Cady Stanton and Amelia Bloomer favored "Turkish trousers," the soft, flowing pants gathered at the ankle that were worn by women in Turkey and the Middle East. This combination of a shortened dress and flowing trousers became known as the

Bloomer costume, or bloomers after Amelia Bloomer endorsed them in the newspaper she edited.

In the United States, the idea of women wearing pants of any kind caused an immediate and prolonged uproar. Some people felt that if women started dressing in any garment that was bifurcated, or divided in two, like men's pants, they would soon set their sights on other areas of men's domain. Then, they worried, gender roles would fall by the wayside. The editors of the *New York Times* said as much in an editorial about a women's rights convention to be held in September 1852. "These ladies assert their claim to rights, which we of bifurcated raiment are charged with usurping," wrote the editors. "They design to evict us. They will enter per force the walks of fame, and honor, and wealth, we now occupy, to compete with us, and strip us of our present monopoly."

Bloomers did gain some converts in the 1850s, but the backlash was so strong that Amelia Bloomer and her colleagues gave up the fight. Some like-minded women formed the Dress Reform Association in 1857, aiming to win women the right to decide what they would and would not wear. However, the outbreak of the Civil War in 1861 stalled their efforts. Meanwhile, women took solace in a new undergarment that helped to lighten the load of their outfits. The crinoline was a hollow cage that got its

With a crinoline cage under her dress, this woman from the 1860s really could command a room!

amelia jenks bloomer

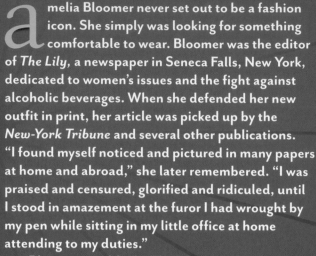

Feminist Amelia Bloomer models the outfit that bore her name in this illustration from 1855.

amelia Bloomer never set out to be a fashion icon. She simply was looking for something comfortable to wear. Bloomer was the editor of *The Lily,* a newspaper in Seneca Falls, New York, dedicated to women's issues and the fight against alcoholic beverages. When she defended her new outfit in print, her article was picked up by the *New-York Tribune* and several other publications. "I found myself noticed and pictured in many papers at home and abroad," she later remembered. "I was praised and censured, glorified and ridiculed, until I stood in amazement at the furor I had wrought by my pen while sitting in my little office at home attending to my duties."

Bloomer would edit *The Lily* until 1855, when she and her husband moved to Council Bluffs, Iowa. In her new home, she continued to work for women's causes. Bloomer served as president of the Iowa Woman Suffrage Society in the 1870s, and she helped to reverse state laws that put a woman's income and property under her husband's control when she married. She died at age 76 in 1894, just as a new generation of women was exploring the benefits of an updated version of bloomers in the age of the bicycle.

round shape from a series of hoops made of steel wire. Emanating from the waist, it gave a woman's dress such diameter that it was impossible for her to walk through a doorway with another person, or even to share a couch with anyone. But it weighed much less than layers of petticoats, and that seemed a step in the right direction.

In 1881, as women in the United States continued to struggle with hoops and corsets and other fashion architecture, their counterparts in England formed the Rational Dress Society. This society called for more reasonable clothing solutions, including limiting the weight of a woman's undergarments to seven pounds. The group's leader, Lady Harberton, introduced a divided skirt, a garment that looked like a skirt, but actually had a separate compartment for each leg. This skirt was slow to catch on, though eventually it would become a popular choice for cyclists in both England and the United States.

BY the 1890s, the growing cycling craze had brought the idea of rational dress front and center. Repeated injuries to women riding in long, full skirts propelled female cyclists to look for new clothing options and others to at least consider the need for them. But for every suggestion of a cycling outfit that was comfortable and safe, there seemed to be a corresponding warning to women not to overstep their bounds. An 1893 article in *Sporting Life* about an incident in New York captured this dichotomy perfectly. "Nearly two years ago we began advocating the adoption of a sensible and rational form of dress for wheelwomen," the article begins. "While we were and are sincere . . . we do not advocate nor will not support any effort on the part of that class of female who seeks to use the wheel as a method to ride into notoriety." What notorious crime had the subject of this article committed? After riding in a park, she had walked her bicycle through the streets of the city while dressed in bloomers. "We regret to see that cycling has at least one woman who so far forgets her own self-respect as to make a public exhibition of herself," wrote *Sporting Life*.

Indeed, newspapers and magazines of the day contained a mixture of thoughtful articles about cycling dress and condemnations of women whom editors felt had gone too far. But even some of the more thoughtful pieces failed to find many complimentary things to say about bloomers. In 1895, *The Cosmopolitan* magazine carried a nine-page article titled "Bicycling for Women" by Mrs. Reginald de Koven, one of the nation's first female sportswriters. "The question of the proper dress for bicycling is still in doubt," wrote Mrs. de Koven. "In America, the present tendency is toward the adoption of short skirts. In smaller cities like Cleveland, Buffalo, and notably in Chicago and Boston, the bloomer costume has been largely used. This tendency must be deprecated. They are a slight gain in convenience, but there is an enormous loss of the gracefulness which every woman should religiously consider."

That same year, the very concept of bloomers caused the Board of School Trustees in the village of College Point, New York, to take an unusual vote. It seems that three female teachers in the village school system made a practice of riding their bicycles to work, and the trustees were aghast. So they voted to prohibit female teachers from riding to and from school. "It is not the proper thing for the ladies to ride the bicycle," Dr. A. F. W. Reimer, one of the trustees, told the *New York Times*. "They wear skirts, of course, but if we do not stop them now they will want to be in style with the New York women and wear bloomers. Then how would our schoolrooms look with the lady teachers parading about among the boys and girls wearing bloomers . . . . We are determined to stop our teachers in time, before they go that far."

No bloomers here! Cyclists in traditional dress take a break in this 1896 illustration showing the latest French fashions for women awheel.

Brooklyn Eagle (Brooklyn, New York)

MARCH 25, 1895

Drew the Line at Bloomers

British Columbia Police Object to a Woman's Bicycle Costume

Victoria, B.C., March 25 — The police have decided that bloomers are not suitable for street wear, even when worn as a bicycling costume, and have taken steps to enforce this decision. Miss Ethel Delmont is an enthusiastic wheel woman, pretty and graceful. Last week she made her appearance in the bloomer costume and if Lady Godiva had herself essayed a repetition of her famous ride the sensation could not have been greater. The town came forth to gaze, and for the moment the police were petrified with amazement. Then they were aroused to action and Miss Ethel was informed that a repetition of her appearance in that costume would mean a police court summons on the charge of creating a disturbance on the public street.

Omaha Daily Bee (Omaha, Nebraska)

OCTOBER 13, 1895

In Favor of Bloomers

A San Francisco merchant, who has been looking at the daily swarm of bicyclers on the boulevard and in Central park, declares in the *New York Sun* that he is astonished at the popular disturbance over the bloomer question in New York. "Why, you don't know anything about bloomers here," he says. "Not one in a hundred of the women who use wheels here is wearing the mannish garment. It is exactly the opposite in San Francisco. Not more than one in fifty of the wheeling women wear skirts when riding. Then again, I notice that you inveigh against bloomers on the score of modesty. Well, in San Francisco the boot is on the other foot. Our more modest women suffer from such constant and strong winds upon the heights and in the park by the Golden Gate, where alone there is level ground for wheeling, that skirts are impossible garments. They cannot be kept down, and therefore, the women have to wear something that will not be blown about. We have become so accustomed to them that we no longer take sides upon the question at their fitness. Instead, we are unanimous in our admiration of a pretty woman in a stylish and well-fitting bloomer costume."

In 1897, a British woman in rational dress brilliantly communicates the joy of cycling in the park.

Despite such instances of civic and journalistic contempt, bloomers got an endorsement of sorts from the Pope Manufacturing Company, makers of Columbia bicycles. Pope started using images of women wearing bloomers in its advertisements in 1894, and the following year the company introduced a set of six paper dolls with cycling costumes, including bloomers, designed by leading dress reformers.

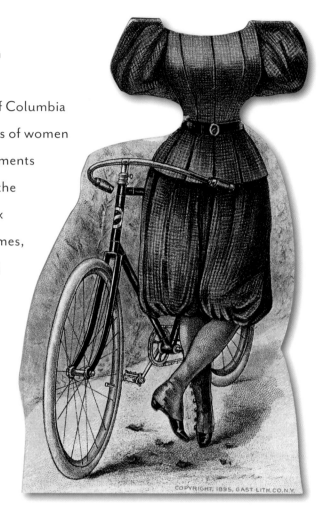

"Some of the most valuable suggestions for costumes for lady cyclists that have appeared this season have emanated from the publishing department of the Pope Manufacturing Company," wrote the *New York Times*. "They are made in paper-doll form. . . .They are purely practical, and are a valuable aid to the lady cyclist in determining the style of her riding habit." The company promised to mail the complete set of dolls to anyone who sent five 2-cent stamps to Pope's Hartford, Connecticut, headquarters.

Besides helping cyclists plan their wardrobes, the Pope Manufacturing Company promised its paper dolls would succeed in "delighting the hearts of all the children into whose hands they may come."

As female cyclists continued to choose from a variety of styles for their wheeling outfits, images of women in bloomers entered popular culture in some surprising ways. More than a few songwriters paid homage to "Pretty Girls

in Bloomers."
(See pages 56-57
for more on bicycle
songs.) Cigar makers
launched brands with
the word "bloomers" in their
names, and the female cyclists on
cigar box labels often wore them. Many
were shown as decidedly masculine, wearing
men's hats, with hair cut short or pulled back, and
smoking cigars, then an almost exclusively male pursuit.
This portrayal reflected the old fears that women in pants would
somehow supplant men as breadwinners and decision-makers.
Only now, some 45 years after the first bloomer "threat," men
seemed to be poking fun at themselves as well as at women.

for their part, more and more

women were rejecting bloomers for cycling. Instead, they wore
shorter skirts. According to an 1896 article in the magazine *Harper's
Bazar*, women in New York and the East were taking the lead in this fashion
trend and for a very clear reason. "Women are too anxious about their personal
appearance to be willing to wear what their own eyes tell them is ugly," the article
said, "and though it took a little time to discover it, this was the unfortunate
adjective which nearly always applied to bloomers." The magazine did say that
even though bloomers were "not desirable" as an outside garment, they were much
better than petticoats for cyclists to wear under their skirts.

Though bloomers enjoyed only a limited rebirth as cycling costumes, they did
live on as uniforms to be worn in physical education classes at women's colleges.

OUR LATEST

O.L.SCHWENCKE.LITH. N.Y.

While the woman at the center of this cigar box label is dressed in the least traditional clothing, the others also are quite modern, with shortened dresses and, in the case of the cyclist on the right, a tie.

But the bicycle craze had a more lasting impact on women's clothing than just the use of bloomers. Thanks in large part to cycling, the innovations of rational dress reformers were starting to take effect by the end of the 1890s. Corsets were on their way out, dresses were getting shorter, and women no longer wore the heavy, bulky undergarments that gave them round, unnatural shapes. These changes went a long way toward unburdening women and setting the stage for them to be healthier and more active in the coming century.

CYCLING SONGS

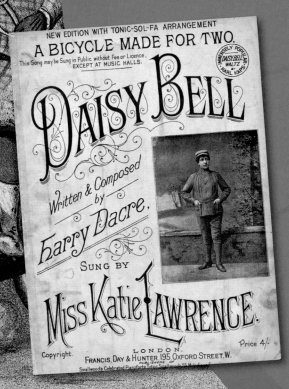

Most middle- and upper-class homes had a piano in the 1890s, and families and friends often gathered around it to sing or listen to songs. Composers produced sheet music at a frantic rate, with the top tunes selling a million copies or more. Not surprisingly, many of them were about the bicycle.

Give Me Your Answer, Do—"Daisy Bell," more commonly known as "A Bicycle Built for Two," is the only turn-of-the-century bicycle song that has stood the test of time. Written in 1892 by English composer Harry Dacre, this romantic tune expresses a man's love for the "beautiful Daisy Bell" and promises that the couple will go "ped'ling away down the road of life" on a "bicycle built for two."

Take That!—British tunesmiths George Le Brun and J. P. Harrington wrote "Salute My Bicycle!" for singer Marie Lloyd in 1895. (Images from the sheet music are at far left and right.) In the chorus, a female cyclist complains that "the fellows all chi-ike"—or jeer—when they see her on her "bike." But she remains "cool as an icicle" and defiantly tells them to "salute my bicycle!"

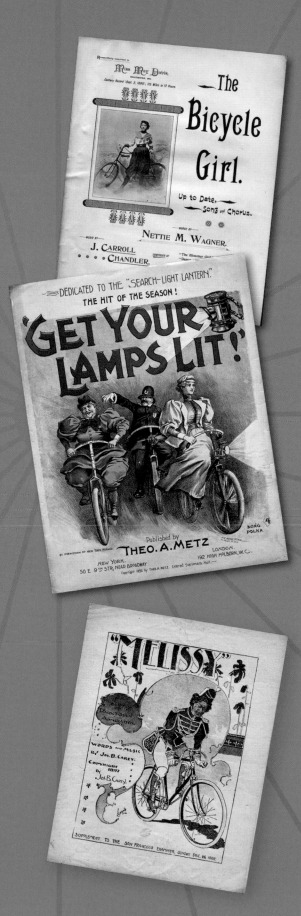

Musical Tribute—Nettie M. Wagner and J. Carroll Chandler dedicated their 1895 song "The Bicycle Girl" to "Miss May Davis," who had earned a century medal by riding 115 miles in 12 hours on September 2 of that year. A photograph of Davis looking proud and comfortable in her bloomer costume graces the cover of the sheet music.

Shedding Some Light—Alarmed by a rise in nighttime bicycle accidents, a number of American cities passed laws requiring cyclists to have lights on their machines. "Get Your Lamps Lit," an 1895 polka by Theo A. Metz, contrasts the fate of Miss Wise, who "was all right for she had a search light," and Miss Foolish, who was fined because she rode without one.

Queen of the Wheel—During the late 19th century, references to African Americans in popular culture used terms that today are unthinkable. One example is the labeling of any neighborhood inhabited mostly by blacks as "Darktown." In the 1897 song "Melissy," composer Joseph B. Carey painted an admiring picture of a young woman who leads the "Darktown Ladies' Cycling Club." She is, he wrote, "the little Queen I love. Spinning along, laughter and song, always jolly, just as bright as any star above."

Background: Detail from the sheet music for "Salute My Bicycle!"

> *It is only a matter of time before one of these women drops dead on her bicycle, and I suppose that that will cause such a hue and cry that contests of this sort will be stopped.*

FEMALE TRAINER OF LONG-DISTANCE CYCLIST JANE LINDSAY
New-York Tribune, October 18, 1899

fast aND

SHORTLY BEFORE 10 A.M. ON THURSDAY, December 23, 1886, Louise Armaindo went flying through the air and landed in a heap. Armaindo, the "champion lady bicyclist of the world," was in the fourth day of a six-day cycling race against two male challengers. But stealing only an occasional hour or two of sleep during short breaks had caught up with her. As Armaindo pedaled her ordinary around the one-eighth-mile track in Minneapolis, Minnesota, her eyelids drooped, and she nodded off. That sent her wobbling high wheeler straight into the fence that surrounded the racing oval, throwing Armaindo over the front wheel and outside the track. "When an assistant arrived she was wide awake, and laughing to herself to think what a figure she must have cut as over the fence she

fearless

In an illustration from 1891, four colorfully — and scantily — dressed women on ordinaries race in front of an appreciative crowd.

Elsa von Blumen poses for a picture on her bicycle. During a race in 1889, the *Pittsburg Dispatch* reported, "Miss von Blumen's style is to a great extent very laborious, but when she leans forward for a spurt her bicycle seems to fly around the track."

flew," reported the *St. Paul Daily Globe.* Unhurt, Armaindo remounted her bicycle and gave chase to her two opponents, riding for almost two and a half hours before leaving the oval to rest and eat. Although she ultimately lost the race, she rode a total of 1,050 miles, the third-longest distance ever for a woman in a six-day contest.

Bicycle racing began in the United States almost as soon as Colonel Albert Pope put the country's first high wheeler on the market in 1878. Cycle makers saw contests of speed and endurance as an excellent way to promote the use of their machines. While the vast majority of racers were men, some women joined the fray, among them Armaindo, a 5'2½" French Canadian, and her frequent rival, Elsa von Blumen of Rochester, New York. Von Blumen, for one, saw herself as a role model, especially for other females. "In presenting myself to the public in my bicycle exercises," she told *The Bicycling World* magazine in 1881, "I feel I am not only offering the most novel and fascinating entertainment now before the people, but am demonstrating the great need of American young ladies, especially, of physical

Founded in 1881, the Springfield (Massachusetts) Bicycle Club held its second annual International Bicycle Meet in 1883, drawing more than 20,000 spectators to its races.

culture and bodily exercise. Success in life depends as much upon a vigorous and healthy body as upon a clear and active mind."

Harper's Weekly, a newspaper that pioneered the use of illustrations alongside text, featured this image of female velocipede racers in Paris in its December 19, 1868, edition.

In the 1880s and '90s, Armaindo, von Blumen, and other female racers took on all comers, including men, horses, and even the occasional dog. They pedaled on the road and on specially built tracks, for short distances and long, competing for money or prizes or glory. Many sustained injuries—at a race in 1891, five of the six female competitors had previously suffered at least one broken arm—but they kept coming back. And more often than not, these racers attracted large crowds and legions of devoted fans while they made their mark as some of the first competitive female athletes in the United States.

races took place throughout the nation, with the East Coast and Midwest proving especially hospitable to female riders. When a troupe of "lady bicyclists" descended upon Minneapolis, Minnesota, for a six-day marathon in 1891, the entire Twin Cities area seemed captivated. Eight days before the start of the race, the *St. Paul Daily Globe* began profiling the women, offering brief descriptions of them and their past achievements. Louise Armaindo, the paper declared, had "the best record in the world among women as an all-round athlete," including the ability to lift 760 pounds "without shoulder straps."

Lillie Williams, of Omaha, Nebraska, was the 18-hour racing champion of America and had won several contests during recent trips to England and France. Teenager May Allen, of Pittsburg, Pennsylvania, also had raced successfully in England. The three remaining cyclists in the field were equally accomplished. Helen Baldwin, a New Yorker with "very large dark-brown eyes, and a decided beauty, both in form and figure," had won a number of 18- and 24-hour races. Aggie Harvey, another Pittsburg native and "the only blonde beauty in the tournament," was not yet 18 but had proven to be a very fast sprinter. And finally, New Yorker Frankie Nelson had a string of sprint and marathon triumphs—including one against two men on roller skates—and had won a six-day race in Detroit just two weeks earlier.

Billed as "in all probability the greatest event in the history of Northwestern cycling," the Minneapolis contest began at 8 p.m. on May 5. The women were to ride around the indoor oval track at Washington rink three hours each night for a total of 18 hours, with the win going to the one who accumulated the most miles. Spectators saw a tight race from the start, with Frankie Nelson racking up 44 miles and just edging out Louise Armaindo and Lillie Williams as the first night ended. Nelson retained the lead on day two, but the real drama involved Williams, who took a header rounding a corner and was knocked unconscious. Only a few minutes after coming to, Williams rushed back on her high wheeler and rode nine more miles until the pain from her injuries grew too great. The doctor on call determined that she had broken her collarbone and left shoulder and couldn't continue. Now it was up to Armaindo to give Nelson a run for her money, and she did, staying within one lap of her through night four. But then Armaindo became ill. Even so, she "rode like a wild woman for at least an hour and a half" on night five, finally tiring and falling to fourth place. In the end, Nelson was victorious, riding 264 miles and 2 laps and beating Williams's previous 18-hour record by more

Sporting Life (Philadelphia, Pennsylvania)

SEPTEMBER 1892

Commentaries

There are many men who contest the title of father of American cycling, but there are no women who want to debate the claims of Louise Armaindo's right to be called the mother of it. Louise was the first in the saddle, the first in the pockets of maker and public alike, and the first to claim for herself the proud title of "lady cyclist." Louise raced men, women, horses, sheriffs, Ecks and almost everything else that thought it had any chance to do this fair and gentle queen of cycling.

To-day the ex-queen of the cinder path races back and forth through the length of a Minneapolis restaurant in the humble guise of a waiter "girl." No longer comes to her shell-like ears the wild roar of the hayreubens as Armaindo defeats a wind-broken, spavin-legged trotter, or casts odium and gravel upon a defeated woman competitor. Gone are those days of glory, gold and get there, and in their places cycling's ex-queen races to the kitchen of a cheap restaurant for "one in the dark" or "slaughter in the pan."

How sad is the sight of fallen and forgotten royalty?

Note: "Ecks" refers to Tom Eck, a bicycle racer and race promoter who Armaindo married.

Many indoor bicycle tracks, such as this one at Madison Square Garden circa 1895, were made of wood and had banked sides that helped riders move more successfully through the turns.

Daily Alta California
(San Francisco, California)

APRIL 14, 1884

Horse and Man Power

To-day at noon the six-day race between Prince and Armaindo, the bicyclists, and Anderson, the mustang rider, will commence. The race is to continue for six days, riding from noon to midnight each day. Armaindo and Prince are to relieve each other every hour, and Anderson has the privilege of changing horses whenever he pleases, but is limited to the use of 15 horses. He has selected tough, small, half-breed horses, and will ride in a common California saddle. The seats in the Pavilion have all been moved and a seven-lap track laid out for Anderson, and a track inside for the bicycle riders. Anderson feels sure of success. He is a plucky young fellow, and has time and again demonstrated remarkable endurance in the saddle. Prince is the prince of bicycle riders, and has had previous experience in this kind of racing, but has never before met California horses and riders. Louise Armaindo is a living example of woman's physical equality with man, having won the championship against men. The managers appear to understand their business, and the race should prove very interesting.

Louise Armaindo was one of the few female cyclists to race both ordinaries and safeties. Before she raced bicycles, she was a noted pedestrienne, or endurance walker, competing in marathon walking races. In the race highlighted in this news article, Prince and Armaindo combined to cover 1,073 miles and one lap, outdistancing Anderson and his horses by one mile and four laps.

than two miles. Harvey was second with 259 miles and 3 laps, followed by Allen with 257 miles and 7 laps, Armaindo with 224 miles and 7 laps, and Baldwin with 178 miles and 3 laps.

Bicycle racing on an indoor track could be a thrilling sport for spectators, who sat outside the oval, so close to the cyclists that they could see their sweat. More than 7,000 people watched the night Frankie Nelson set her 18-hour record in Minneapolis, and a good number of those in the stands were female. "Men go to see what their brothers can do in the way of athletics," the *St. Paul Daily Globe* pointed out during that race. "Why shouldn't women be interested in their sisters?" But while Frankie Nelson and company were burning rubber on indoor tracks in front of thousands of adoring fans, others were braving the uneven roads outdoors, virtually alone. One woman in particular, a married mother of three in her early 20s, declared in 1894 that she would ride her bicycle as far as a person could go — around the world.

for annie cohen kopchovsky, cycling

around the world was just one more challenge in a life where nothing came easy. Born near Riga, in Eastern Europe, Annie Cohen immigrated to the United States with her family when she was just four or five years old. The family settled in Boston. By the time she was 17, both of her parents had died, and she and her older brother were responsible for raising their two younger siblings. Annie married Max Kopchovsky, a peddler, when she was 18 and soon started a family of her own. She also started selling advertising space for various newspapers. Kopchovsky's skill at sales came in handy in 1894, when she purportedly heard about a wager that two wealthy men had made. According to her account, the men disagreed on whether or not a woman could ride a bicycle around the world, as American Thomas Stevens had done in the 1880s. They stipulated that

In this somewhat somber portrait, Annie Kopchovsky poses with the lady's cycle that she rode on the first legs of her journey.

the cyclist had to start with no money, and that she had to return with at least $5,000 she earned along the way. Although Kopchovsky had never even ridden a bicycle, she decided that she was the woman for the job.

After two quick lessons, Kopchovsky was ready to head out of Boston on her new 42-pound Columbia lady's cycle. Before leaving, though, she accepted one hundred dollars from a sponsor, the Londonderry Lithia Spring Water Company of New Hampshire. The company got a lot for the money. Not only did Annie place an advertising sign on her bicycle, she also changed her name to Annie Londonderry for the duration of the trip! Finally, on June 25, 1894, she was off. She pedaled to New York, over good roads and bad, in eight days, but with stops to rest and earn money, she didn't reach Chicago, Illinois, until September 24. It had taken her three months to travel approximately 1,300 miles, and she had more than 20,000 miles left to cover.

Annie Londonderry thought about giving up, but instead made some changes, trading her heavy skirts for bloomers and her Columbia bike for a much lighter men's Sterling. She also decided to head east, riding back to New York and crossing the Atlantic on an ocean liner. Annie traveled largely by ship through Europe, the Mideast, and Asia, taking short cycling trips at various points along the route. She reached San Francisco, California, on March 23, 1895, and pedaled to Chicago to complete the journey. When she arrived on September 12, 1895, she had indeed earned $5,000 by selling souvenirs, taking more advertising, and giving lectures and cycling demonstrations. Along the way, Annie had become quite a celebrity. Several businesses, including the Sterling Bicycle Company, had signed her up to promote their products, and the *New York World* ran her own account of the journey on the front page of its October 20, 1895, edition.

Annie Londonderry wasn't the only one who pushed the limits of time and distance on her two-wheeler. In the late 1890s, several women took the concept of riding a century — 100 miles — to the extreme by peeling off two, three, four, or more

In an advertising card celebrating female bicycle racers (shown front and back), the New Brunswick Tire Company cautions, "racing is risky business, unless you are sure of your tire."

DORA RINEHART

ora Rinehart loved her husband, but she didn't necessarily want to ride her bicycle with him. "I don't like to go on a hard run when my husband is with me," she told *The Cycling West* magazine in 1897. "For you know it does take so much starch out of a man to ride a century, especially if he be not in the best of shape." In her husband's defense, few people could keep up with Rinehart on the bicycle paths. The magazine described her "long rides through rain, darkness, mud, snow and slush," her battles against sandstorms, sleet, and "rain blizzards," and her constant desire to go faster and farther than she had before. "She is an intellectual student of nature," the magazine continued, "a philosopher and a lady of self-possession in whose composition is embodied determination, grit and firmness."

Not surprisingly, Rinehart wasn't afraid to speak her mind. In 1894, she testified at the annual convention of the Colorado State Medical Society about the benefits of the divided skirt for female cyclists. "It is almost impossible for a lady to ride any distance...with the ordinary skirt," she told the mostly male audience. "You get too much of the dress on the one side of the wheel, and you do not get enough of the dress on the other side." Rinehart's success brought her a number of product endorsements, including Stearns bicycles, Samson tires, and the Rinehart Skirt, a divided skirt designed in her honor by a seamstress in Denver.

In 1897, *The Cycling West* called the five-foot-one, 140-pound Rinehart "Denver's petite but Herculean mistress of the road."

centuries in a row. Perhaps the greatest female century rider performed outside the spotlight. Dora Rinehart's exploits hardly ever were reported beyond the western United States, where the Colorado native earned the title "America's Greatest Cyclienne." Rinehart took up the bicycle to regain her strength after suffering from scarlet fever. She started with short rides, but quickly built up her endurance. In 1896 alone, she pedaled 17,196 miles, more than any other woman in the United States. That included stretches of 10 days in July and 20 days from October 31 through November 19 when she rode a century every day.

SOON *after* RINEHART REWROTE THE RECORD

books, a battle of dueling century riders in Long Island, New York, attracted national attention. Irene Brush of Brooklyn started things off by pedaling 200 miles in 22 hours on May 7 and 8, 1899. A month later, she rode 300 miles in 29 hours and in mid-July, 400 miles in 48 hours. Brush's achievements soon were eclipsed by two new marathon cyclists. In late July, Jane Yatman, a 24-year-old former bookstore clerk from Manhattan, powered through five centuries in 58 hours. In early September, Jane Lindsay of Brooklyn pedaled 600 miles in 72 hours. Later that month, on September 16, Jane Yatman set out to ride 700 miles, a feat which she accomplished in 81 hours, 5 minutes. "Miss Yatman plainly showed the effects of the terrible strain in her countenance," reported the *New York Times,* "and said that the ride was torture during the last twenty-five miles." Those miles, and indeed the entire last century, were ridden in a drenching rainstorm.

Yatman had little time to savor her ownership of the Long Island women's century record, as Jane Lindsay responded with an even longer ride. On October 18, Lindsay completed an 800-mile marathon in 91 hours, 48 minutes. Upon reporting Lindsay's newest feat, the *New York Times* pointed out that there was no monetary reward for such "useless and necessarily injurious trials of strength" and suggested what the women's motivation might be. "Bitter rivalry, that characteristic feminine

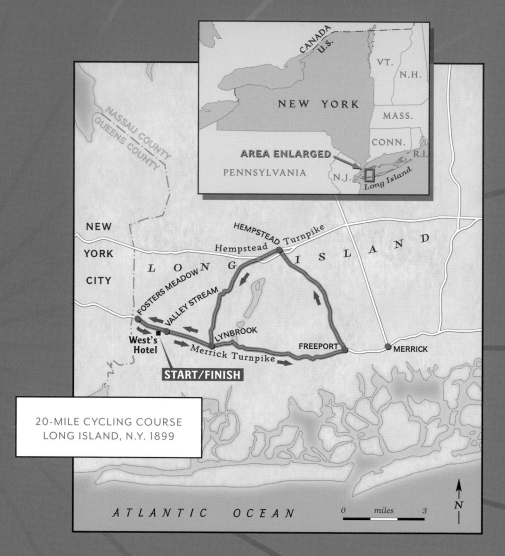

**20-MILE CYCLING COURSE
LONG ISLAND, N.Y. 1899**

West's Hotel was the headquarters for Jane Yatman, Jane Lindsay, and other cyclists who attempted century runs on Long Island. During their 1899 rivalry, the two Janes stopped there for short naps, small meals, and lots of liquid refreshment, including tea, milk, broth, and sometimes beer. When Jane Lindsay rode her 800-mile marathon, she dismounted at West's after every 100 miles to take a bath, get a massage, and put on fresh undergarments.

Jane Yatman never challenged Jane Lindsay's 800-mile record. Instead, she found a new venue for her long-distance cycling. In 1900, she rode from New York to Chicago—approximately 1,050 miles—in 254 hours and 40 minutes.

trait, and the determination to 'get even' are seemingly the actuating motives," wrote the *Times*. Lindsay's actions certainly support the impression that a rivalry existed. Both she and Yatman rode the same 20-mile course in Long Island, New York, over and over again in their century quests, and both stayed at West's Hotel in Valley Stream, Long Island, when they were through. The hotel had a sign in the main room commemorating Yatman's 700-mile ride until Lindsay tore it down and tossed it aside, replacing it with one of her own. The new sign proclaimed: "Champion! Unexcelled — Unapproached. Jane Lindsay."

Despite their determination and daring, female bicycle athletes didn't always have the support of the cycling community. In 1896, *Sporting Life* applauded what the newspaper saw as the failure of a recent six-day women's bicycle race in New York City, declaring, "This ensures that the disgusting and degrading exhibition will not soon be repeated. Woman's place in cycling is not on the public race path." In 1897, the League of American Wheelmen, which regulated races, included in its bylaws the statement, "No race meeting shall receive official sanction if it . . . has upon its schedule any event which is open to women competitors." Local officials sometimes made things difficult for female road racers as well. In 1900, another marathoner, Marguerite Gast, set out to pedal around Long Island for at least 4,500 miles. She had covered 2,600 miles in 12 days, 7 hours, and 55 minutes when the sheriff stopped her. He said he was acting on the orders of the Nassau County district attorney, who considered it "improper, immoral, and illegal to make such an exhibition on the public highway."

Sporting Life, the L.A.W., and the Nassau County district attorney all seemed determined to impose limits on the new freedoms that the bicycle made possible for women. But they were too late. With millions of women embracing the safety in the 1890s, there was no putting on the brakes.

the cycling PRESS

When Americans took to the wheel in the late 1800s, they also took to the newsstand. The first U.S. cycling periodical, *Bicycling World*, rolled off the presses in 1877, a year before Colonel Albert Pope introduced his Columbia high wheeler. By 1894, there were more than 50 cycling publications to choose from stateside and many more around the world.

THE AMERICAN *Wheelman*

NEW YORK, BUFFALO & CHICAGO.

WOMAN AWHEEL.

A PLEASANT HOUR

Every week The American Wheelman is filled with the Brightest Woman's Matter from the pens of the best women writers on cycling in America. It is the only cycling paper that makes a specialty of this.

Our special illustrations and articles go to make The American Wheelman the woman's favorite.

INK & TAYLOR COLL.

FOR SALE HERE.
Price, 10 Cents.

Mammoth Magazine—In 1896, a 308-page edition of *The American Wheelman* earned the distinction of being "the largest magazine ever issued from a printing press," according to the advertising journal *Printers' Ink.* Considered one of the "big four" cycling magazines, along with *Bearings, The Wheel,* and *The Referee, The American Wheelman* apparently had so much bicycle news to share that for a while, it was published daily.

N·ILLUSTRATED·JOURNA

Bearing With It—Although the earliest cycling magazines in the United States were published on the East Coast, Chicago entered the fray in the mid-1880s with *Bearings* and *The Referee.* Both struggled until the growing popularity of the safety helped drive up their circulation. In 1896, *Printers' Ink* declared that *Bearings* was "the only weekly magazine in the world running near the number of pages seen each week between its green covers."

It's the L.A.W.—Good roads were such a priority for the League of American Wheelmen that in August 1895, the group merged its official publication with *Good Roads* magazine to produce *The L.A.W. Bulletin and Good Roads.* This weekly campaigned heavily for road improvements but also reported on the activities of L.A.W. members and on events held by cycling clubs.

A Voice for Women—While many cycling magazines included a smattering of articles aimed at women, *The Wheelwoman* was one of the few devoted exclusively to that audience. Launched in 1895 as "The Bicycling Authority for Women," it promised "instructive and interesting articles on the subject upon which the existing cycling press is almost unanimously silent."

Background: Detail from the cover of the British cycling magazine, *The Hub*

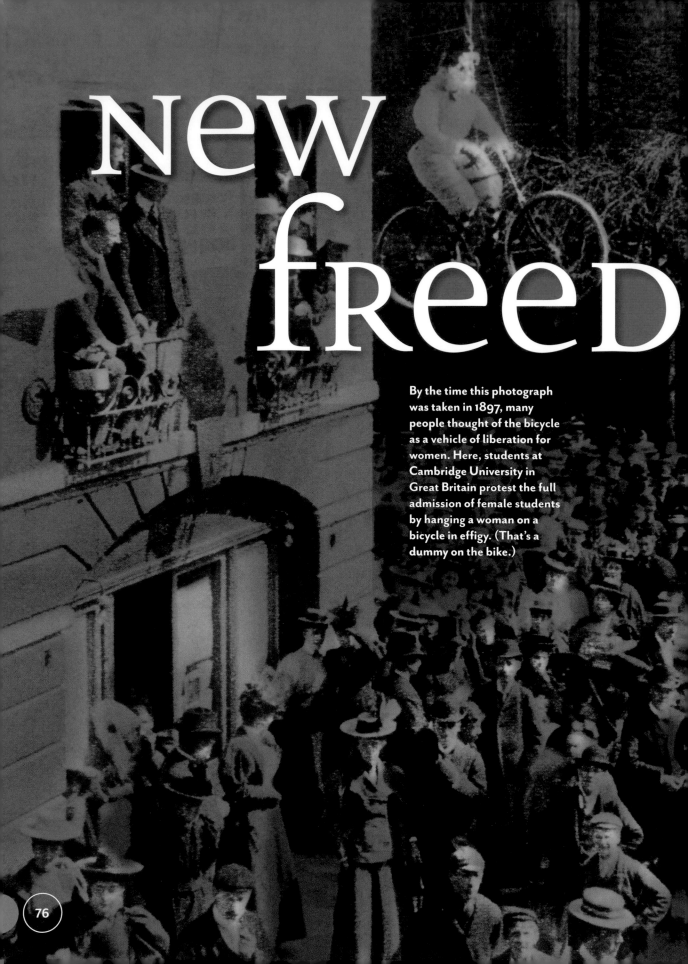

New freed

By the time this photograph was taken in 1897, many people thought of the bicycle as a vehicle of liberation for women. Here, students at Cambridge University in Great Britain protest the full admission of female students by hanging a woman on a bicycle in effigy. (That's a dummy on the bike.)

> *"Let me tell you what I think of bicycling. I think it has done more to emancipate women than anything else in the world. I stand and rejoice every time I see a woman ride by on a wheel."*

SUSAN B. ANTHONY IN "CHAMPION OF HER SEX,"
BY NELLIE BLY • *New York World*, February 2, 1896

oms

WOMEN'S RIGHTS CRUSADER ELIZABETH

Cady Stanton was in her eighties during the heyday of the bicycle, and no evidence exists to show that she actually ever rode one. But there was no better or more eloquent advocate for women and the wheel. In 1895, Stanton contributed an article to the *American Wheelman* celebrating this "wonderful new style of locomotion." In the article, titled "The Era of the Bicycle," she pointed out that cycling was increasing people's mobility, eliminating the cost of feeding and housing horses, and encouraging the building of good roads. However, she saved her greatest praise for the bicycle's effects on women. "The bicycle," she wrote, "will inspire women with more courage, self-respect and self-reliance and make the next generation more vigorous of mind and of body; for feeble mothers do not produce great statesmen, scientists and scholars."

For all the practical benefits of the two-wheeler, the fact is that it brought about a cosmic shift in women's private and public lives. With the rise of industry and the move from a rural to an urban economy in the 19th century, American women had become increasingly confined to their homes. Young girls could play outside, but when they matured, their freedom of movement was greatly restricted. "At sixteen years of age, I was enwrapped in the long skirts that impeded every footstep," remembered Frances Willard, who in 1895 wrote a best-selling account of how she learned to ride a bicycle at age 53. "I have detested walking and felt with a certain noble disdain that the conventions of life had cut me off from what . . . had been one of life's sweetest joys."

While wealthier women were saddled with long skirts and restrictive corsets, those who were less well off worked anonymously in mills and factories. All in all, the result was the same. Except in a few instances, the public image of America was male. Politicians, soldiers, business leaders, and even the leading athletes in the new sports of baseball and football were all men. But the bicycle changed that. Suddenly, women were leaving their homes to cycle and socialize on country roads and city streets. Bicycle racers such as Louise Armaindo and Frankie Nelson had their exploits splashed all over the papers. Bicycle manufacturers, intent on mining an untapped market, showed female models in their advertisements. Thanks to the wheel, women were starting to be seen and heard in public life.

It was not a stretch for some cyclists to see the possibility of a larger role for women in the world. When she conquered the wheel, Frances Willard was a former university president and the longtime president of the Woman's Christian Temperance Union, which fought

frances willard

What possessed Frances Willard to learn to ride a bicycle at age 53? She did it for her health, she wrote, and for the "pure love of nature." She also wanted to inspire other women to learn to ride: "I hold that the more interests women and men can have in common, in thought, word, and deed, the happier it will be for the home." Finally, she declared that she did it "because a good many people thought I could not do it at my age."

It's hard to believe that anyone could doubt Willard's ability to do anything she set her mind to. Spurred at least in part by her brother's battle with alcoholism, Willard helped to found the Woman's Christian Temperance Union (WCTU) and became its president in 1879. In that capacity, she vowed to visit every town in the United States with a population of 10,000 or more to speak about the evils of alcohol. Over a period of 10 years, she averaged one public address per day, effectively spreading her message throughout the country. When she died of influenza in 1898, the *New York Times* wrote, "She possessed that unknown quantity often called magnetism, which was felt in her private conversation as well as in her public addresses. She had an equable temper, a ready wit, and a great fund of humor."

Frances Willard depended on these "three young Englishmen," among others, to teach her how to ride a bicycle. She wrote that to fully master the machine she practiced an average of 15 minutes per day for about three months.

79

Elizabeth Cady Stanton, left, and Susan B. Anthony, right, were united in both their appreciation of the bicycle and their dedication to women's suffrage.

to prohibit the use of alcoholic beverages and to win women the right to vote. Willard saw parallels between learning to ride and learning to live. "I began to feel that myself plus the bicycle equaled myself plus the world, upon whose spinning wheel we must all learn to ride," she wrote. "He who succeeds, or, to be more exact in handing over my experience, she who succeeds in gaining the mastery of [a bicycle], will gain the mastery of life."

For decades, Willard, along with Elizabeth Cady Stanton, Susan B. Anthony, and many others, had been working toward increased political and economic rights for women. Now the bicycle brought a taste of independence to women on a very personal level, and some of them took the opportunity to express their discontent with old traditions and expectations. In August 1895, a cyclist named Ann Strong caused a stir when she compared the value of a bicycle to that of a husband in the *Minneapolis Tribune*. "I can't see but that a wheel is just as good company as most husbands," she declared. "I would as lief [*sic*] talk to one inanimate object as another; and I'd a great deal rather talk to one that can't answer than one that won't." Strong then contrasted the joy of cycling with the challenges of raising a family. "You can make your wheel tidy over night," she said, "and it never kicks off its shoes the very last minute, and never smears itself with molasses.

When you are ready you can start. No little elbows are stuck in your ribs; there is no wiggling; screams at the cars or at the candy stores. You glide along, silently, smoothly, swiftly."

Some stated the liberating effects of the bicycle with less sarcasm. "The bicycle has brought to women a healthful, wholesome means of securing a degree of freedom and independence that no amount of discussion regarding 'women's rights' would ever have produced," wrote the *L.A.W. Bulletin and Good Roads* magazine in 1898. Meanwhile, *Munsey's Magazine* assessed the impact of the wheel on women in a special bicycle-themed issue. "If she has ridden her bicycle into new fields, becoming in the process a new creature, it has been gradually and unconsciously," the editors wrote.

Elizabeth Cady Stanton wrote that the bicycle taught "an equality in social relations without distinction as to color or previous conditions of servitude." Although mainstream magazines almost exclusively showed images of white cyclists, African Americans such as this young woman also took to the road.

A woman with wings graces this French cycling poster, circa 1900.

"She did not have to be born again in some mysterious fashion, becoming a strange creature, a 'new woman.' She is more like the 'eternal feminine,' who has taken on wings, and who is using them with an ever increasing delight in her new power." Indeed, many bicycle companies at home and abroad did put wings on the women in their advertisements, emphasizing that they had taken flight.

Not all publications treated the emergence of the "new woman" with the same level of approval. Some mocked her, while others just seemed baffled by her. Her new way of dressing, in bloomers or divided skirts or skirts with shortened hems, certainly disturbed the old social order, but so did her confidence and daring. These traits led commentators to worry that the differences between the sexes were being blurred, a fear that was reinforced as the four newest states—Wyoming, Colorado, Utah, and Idaho—granted women the right to vote in the 1890s. Would the bicycle help bring about a new kind of equality between men and women? Elizabeth Cady Stanton and her colleagues certainly hoped so. At any rate, the image of a female cyclist quickly became associated with efforts to win more rights for women. When Cambridge University in England decided to offer female students full admission in 1897, the male students protested by hanging a figure of a woman on a bicycle in effigy.

POETS AND WRITERS ALSO EXPLORED THE impact of the wheel and the changing dynamics between the sexes that it helped bring about. Magazines and some newspapers regularly published poetry and short stories at that time, and cycling was a popular theme. In 1893, poet Madeline S. Bridges celebrated the female cyclist's new freedom by contrasting her with the maidens of the past who used wheels to spin thread:

Wheels and Wheels

The maiden with her wheel of old
Sat by the fire to spin,
While lightly through her careful hold
The flax slid out and in.
Today, her distaff, rock and reel
Far out of sight are hurled,
For now the maiden with her wheel
Goes spinning round the world.

Short stories sometimes aimed to reassure men that women's love of the wheel made them even better companions. In "A Century Ride," by Grace E. Denison,

In this 1880 photograph, a young woman spins yarn from fibers on a spinning wheel.

Maude Mannering, a "successful girl graduate and medical student," is visiting her friend's farm, far from civilization. When another visitor, her former beau, falls and breaks his leg, Maude sets the leg and then hops on her bicycle and rides 50 miles to fetch the doctor, who heads out to the farm on horseback. After a short nap, Maude begins the return trip on her wheel, finishing as dawn is breaking: "Fifty miles there and fifty miles back—a *hundred miles*—A CENTURY! Had not some girl in the South told her she had ridden a century? Ever since that day a little envy had been in her heart of that girl, and she sometimes wished very much that she, too, might wear upon her cycling blouse that tiny bar of gold, with its magic figures, recording a ride of one hundred miles." Maude's valiant, selfless riding so impresses the doctor that a few months later, he marries her.

Edna C. Jackson's story "A Fin de Cycle Incident" focuses more directly on the battle of the sexes brought on by the bicycle. Renie Raine is engaged to be married to Horace P. Waldron, who vehemently disapproves of women who are athletic in any way. Unbeknownst to him, Renie is indeed an athlete, and she readily accepts her brother's offer to teach her to ride a bicycle. During the process, she even starts wearing bloomers, declaring, "I don't see what skirts were made for, anyhow! They are always in the way!" She quickly falls in love with cycling, but her guilt at deceiving her fiancé gnaws at her: "Several times she bravely resolved, since she could not decide between her lover and her wheel, that she would boldly ride, bloomers and blouse, around by his office or his club and reveal to him her offending in all its enormity; but the next day she would weaken." Finally, Renie decides to give up the wheel after taking one last spin through the woods. On her trip, she hears two hoboes plotting to rob and murder Horace, who they know will

Ride a STEARNS and be content

Edward Penfield, considered by many to be the originator of the poster in the United States, designed and illustrated this classic advertisement for Stearns bicycles.

Daily Record-Union (Sacramento, California)

AUGUST 28, 1895

EDITORIAL

The editor of *Harper's Weekly* believes that woman is riding on the bicycle to greater freedom and independence, learning to take care of herself, becoming more self-reliant and generally better. However that may be as a matter of philosophy, it is questionable if it is an advance. All we can do is to wait and see; there will be very speedy results. We make and break customs very rapidly in these days, but we do not believe that the bicycle is to exercise as broad an influence in molding womanly character as *Harper's* seems to think. That it is affecting a change of habit among a great many women is true, and while in some cases it may be beneficial, assuredly in many others it is bad.

New York Times (New York, New York)

JULY 5, 1896

Gossip of the Cyclers

A Wheelwoman's Adventure in Oregon

An Oregon wheelwoman had a thrilling adventure a short time ago which takes the palm for the present season. She is a Portland woman, and was visiting at Roseburg. One day she decided to go on a thirty-mile journey out in the mountains. After wheeling twenty-five miles the road gave out, or rather, she reached the end of it. Finding a trail, she followed it about a mile, when she came to a foot log over a narrow, turbulent stream. Dreading to walk across with her wheel, she decided to ride over, having great confidence in her skill as a cyclist. Of course, her wheel slipped, and both machine and rider tumbled into the water. Being a good swimmer, the lady got out all right, and after a time fished out her wheel. As night was approaching she resumed her journey over the trail without loss of time, hoping to reach her destination while daylight yet remained. What was her horror when she had struck a fast gait to see in the trail ahead of her, and less than 100 yards away, a huge bear, apparently waiting to receive her. Making up her mind instantly what to do, she sprinted the harder, and clanged her bell, bearing down meanwhile on Mr. Bear. The combination feazed [sic] the latter, and just in the nick of time he wheeled out of the path and the daring woman sped on to safety.

A woman with a bicycle appears to burst through the cover of the March 2, 1902, issue of the French sporting magazine, *La Vie au Grand Air*.

86

(*Voir l'article page : 30*).

be passing through that night with a great deal of money that he is collecting for his employer. Renie risks her life on a dramatic ride to warn Horace, just escaping a train that is bearing down on her. Her beloved is so thankful that he takes up cycling himself and spends many happy hours awheel with his athletic hero.

These and other uplifting stories reinforced the notion that the bicycle made women better partners and better citizens. It was an empowering message and one that was perfectly in line with the sentiments of Elizabeth Cady Stanton and her sister suffragists.

As the 1890s drew to a close, the cyclists who had cast off their corsets and taken to the open road were leading the way for American women to start embracing new freedoms and a larger place in public life. Ironically, the vehicle that had delivered them to the future had almost reached the end of the road. By the turn of the century, the bicycle's heyday was over and a new mechanical wonder promised to transport men and women faster and farther than ever before. Bicycle manufacturers retooled their factories to build them and bicycle repair shops installed gasoline tanks to service them. The era of the automobile had begun.

selling
with cycles

As the bicycle craze swept the nation, the advertising industry began using images of cyclists to sell everything from candy to carpets. All of the items shown here, except for the salmon can label, are trade cards. These cards, given out by businesses to attract customers, were especially popular after new technology made color printing possible in the late 1800s. The cards often had a color image on the front and a black-and-white message on the back.

Cycle Brand Salmon, Bellingham, Washington

COMPLIMENTS OF
THE RIDLEY CHAMBERS ST. CANDY MANUFACTORY,
CHAMBERS STREET, COR. HUDSON.

The Ridley Chambers Street Candy Manufactory, New York, New York

GIVEN TO ME BY
Springfield Carpet Co.
PIERIK BUILDING,
East Side Square.

Springfield Carpet Company, Springfield, Illinois

The Northern Milling Co.
CHICAGO.

A ONESIDED RACE
NORTHERN BELLE FLOUR ALWAYS AHEAD.

NORTHERN MILLING COMPANY
DAILY CAPACITY, 2000 BBLS. FLOUR.
MADISON ST. BRIDGE,   CHICAGO, ILLS.
We are grinding the very Choicest Selected Minnesota and Dakota Hard Spring Wheat. Our mills are new and modern, and we guarantee our Patent flour to be superior in every respect to all other flours.
If you want a flour which will give the very best results, make the best bread and the best biscuit, and always of the highest and most uniform quality, then see that the following name is on every barrel or sack of flour you buy:
NORTHERN MILLING CO.
CHICAGO.
Your grocer may try to force upon you some other flour on which he makes more money.
SEND IT BACK. Insist upon having Northern Milling Company's flour.

HINTS ON BREAD MAKING.
Our American women are acknowledged to be the finest cooks in the world, and while we do not presume to give them instructions in the art of bread making, still the following suggestions, if closely observed, will give most excellent results.
Always use good fresh yeast.
Always sift and warm flour before using.
Always keep in a moderately warm place of even temperature while rising.
Always knead thoroughly, the longer the better.
These points are all important, but after all the great secret is to use flour from
NORTHERN MILLING CO., CHICAGO.

The Northern Milling Company, Chicago, Illinois, front and back

Background: Detail from a trade card for the Riverside Yeast Company, Chicago, Illinois

HIGHLIGHTS IN CYCLING AND WOMEN'S HISTORY

1851
Elizabeth Cady Stanton wears an outfit of loose trousers gathered at the ankles and covered by a short skirt on a visit to newspaper editor Amelia Bloomer. After Amelia endorses it, the costume comes to be called bloomers.

1848
Elizabeth Cady Stanton helps to organize a women's rights convention in Seneca Falls, New York. More than 100 delegates sign a Declaration of Rights and Sentiments, which becomes a founding document of the woman's suffrage movement.

1834, 1836
Female textile workers in Lowell, Massachusetts, strike for better conditions. They fail in their attempt to turn back a 15 percent wage cut in 1834, but two years later win their fight against a rent hike in company boardinghouses.

1807
Lawmakers in New Jersey revoke the right of women to vote, which had been guaranteed by the state constitution since 1776. No U.S. state would allow women to vote again until 1890.

1850
1840
1830
1820
1810
1800
1770

BICYCLE HISTORY

1817
Baron Karl von Drais of Germany builds a *laufmaschine* (running machine), or *draisine*, that is propelled by the rider's feet pushing against the ground.

1776
In a letter, Abigail Adams urges her husband, John, and the Continental Congress to "Remember the Ladies" as they write the laws of the new nation, adding, "If particular care and attention is not paid to the ladies we are determined to foment a rebellion."

1819
British coachmaker Denis Johnson introduces an improved version of the draisine called the hobbyhorse and opens a school to teach people to ride it.

WOMEN'S HISTORY

PLAYER'S CIGARETTES

LADY CYCLIST, 1896

"This charming and wasp-waisted lady wheeler of 40 years ago was a member of the aristocracy," states the back of this British collectible card from the 1930s.

1869
Susan B. Anthony and Elizabeth Cady Stanton form the National Woman Suffrage Association to oppose the 15th Amendment to the U.S. Constitution, which extends voting rights to black men but not to women.

1873
Frances Willard helps to found the Woman's Christian Temperance Union to fight for woman's suffrage and other social reforms and against the consumption of alcohol.

1890
Wyoming becomes a state and its constitution grants women the right to vote in all elections. Three years later, the male citizens of Colorado pass a referendum granting full suffrage to women.

1911
A fire at the Triangle Shirtwaist Factory in New York City kills 146 workers, most of them women. The fire leads to stricter laws on factory safety.

1916
Two years after she helps women gain the right to vote in Montana, native daughter Jeanette Rankin wins election to the U.S. House of Representatives, becoming the first woman elected to either house of Congress.

1920
Women gain the right to vote in all U.S. elections with the passage of the 19th Amendment to the Constitution of the United States.

1923
Alice Paul and the National Women's Party propose an Equal Rights Amendment to outlaw discrimination on the basis of sex. Though Congress finally passes it in 1972, it is ratified by only 35 states—three short of the requirement—and never becomes law.

1860   1870   1880   1890   1900   1910   1920

1867
French inventors develop a pedal-driven velocipede that soon earns the nickname boneshaker because its stiff construction and iron wheels shake riders to the core.

1870
England's Starley and Company patents the Ariel, an all-metal velocipede with a large wheel in front and a much smaller one in back. It helps popularize the high-wheel bicycle, also called the ordinary.

1878
Colonel Albert Augustus Pope launches the Pope Manufacturing Company, whose Columbia bicycles are the first ordinaries built in the United States.

1880
Pope and others form the League of American Wheelmen (the L.A.W.) to look out for the interests of cyclists and fight for the improvement of the nation's roads.

1887
A. H. Overman of Chicopee, Massachusetts, builds the Victor Bicycle, with two wheels of equal size. It is the first safety patented in the United States.

1888
John Dunlop of Scotland invents the pneumatic tire, a rubber tire with an inner tube filled with compressed air. It allows for faster, more comfortable rides and ultimately adds to the popularity of the safety.

1895
Ignaz Schwinn and Adolph Arnold form Arnold, Schwinn & Company in Chicago, renamed the Schwinn Bicycle Company in 1967. It would be the top American bicycle manufacturer for much of the 20th century.

1897
After a decade of expansion and overproduction, the American bicycle boom goes bust. Manufacturers sharply reduce prices and some, including the Overman Wheel Company, maker of the first U.S. safeties, close up shop.

1898
Bicycles become motorized when the Waltham Manufacturing Company of Massachusetts introduces the first successful models of American motorcycles. Harley-Davidson and other companies soon enter the field.

Early 1900s
Former bicycle mechanics move on to new technologies. Henry Ford and Charles Duryea start their own automobile companies and Orville and Wilbur Wright and Glenn Curtiss build airplanes.

Resources

BOOKS

Herlihy, David V. *Bicycle: The History*. New Haven, Connecticut: Yale University Press, 2004.

No detail is left unexamined in this comprehensive, lavishly illustrated look at the story of the bicycle from its "pre-history" through the 20th century.

Joselit, Jenna Weissman. *A Perfect Fit: Clothes, Character, and the Promise of America*. New York: Metropolitan Books, 2001.

Read about the changes in women's clothing brought about by the bicycle in the larger context of the evolution of men's and women's fashion from the 1890s through the 1930s.

Smith, Robert A. *A Social History of the Bicycle: Its Early Life and Times in America*. New York: American Heritage Press, 1972.

This classic volume helped establish just how interesting, entertaining, and relevant the history of the bicycle is. And it's a great read.

Zheutlin, Peter. *Around the World on Two Wheels: Annie Londonderry's Extraordinary Ride*. New York: Citadel Press, 2007.

In the process of analyzing his great-grandaunt's dramatic cycling trip around the world, the author shapes a portrait of one gutsy Jewish immigrant and a whole generation of "new women" who rode their bicycles to richer lives.

WEB SITES

Tubulocity: Bicycle Culture for a Tubular World
tubulocity.com

Publisher Eric Shalit keeps this online magazine lively with a mixture of multimedia features on bicycling in the present and the past.

The Wheelmen: Dedicated to the Enjoyment and Preservation of Our Bicycling Heritage
thewheelmen.org

There's much to explore on this site, home of the Wheelmen, a group that celebrates the culture of cycling before 1918. Start with the collection of vintage bicycle-themed sheet music, photographs, ribbons, and cigar box labels, and then check out the pictures of 21st-century cyclists riding bikes from the past. There's also a terrific list of links.

The World Awheel: Early Cycling Books at the Lilly Library
indiana.edu/~liblilly/awheel/awheel.html

This excellent online exhibition from the University of Indiana's Lilly Library covers topics including Cycling in Fiction, Cycling Music, and Women Awheel.

PLACES TO VISIT

Bicycle Museum of America
7 West Monroe Street
New Bremen, Ohio 45869
bicyclemuseum.com

Owned by the grandson of a turn-of-the-20th-century bicycle maker, the museum moved to this small Ohio town from Chicago. *Art & Antiques* magazine chose it as one of the "100 Top Treasures" to see in the United States and Canada.

Metz Bicycle Museum
Freehold, New Jersey 07728
metzbicyclemuseum.com

Among the hundreds of bikes at this museum, there is a rare lamplighter bicycle—an eight-foot-tall cycle that workers rode in 1890s New York City as they lit the gas street lamps. Metz also offers collections of antique children's riding toys, mousetraps, pencil sharpeners, and other items.

sources of quotes

Here are the sources of all the quotations used in this book. A full citation is given the first time a source is mentioned. After that, the citation is abbreviated.

Chapter 1: Inventing the Bicycle
p. 14: Drais's vehicle: *Encyclopædia Britannica* quoted in "Evolution of the Bicycle," *The National Magazine*, November 1892; p. 18: Hough: "A Test Bicycle Case," *New York Times*, July 15, 1881; p. 19: Patents: Kate Parke, Bicycle-Lock, patent #436,800; Alice A. Bennitt. Bicycle-Canopy, #574,235; Mary F. Henderson, Bicycle-Saddle, #572,164 (1896) and #576,310 (1897); Sarah C. Clagett, Bicycle-Skirt Fastener, #578,444; Agness Amess and Maude A. Powlison, Bicycle Stand and Lock, #632,165. All can be found through Google Patents: *google.com/patents?hl=en*; p. 20: "Female Mathew Brady": "Old Friends Honor Miss Alice Austen," *New York Times*, October 8, 1951; p. 21: The L.A.W. Mission: *A Social History of the Bicycle: Its Early Life and Times in America* by Robert A. Smith, New York: American Heritage Press, 1972, p. 12; p. 25: "nearly half a million machines": "Gossip of the Cyclers: How the Wheel-Making Industry Has Grown in a Decade," *New York Times*, April 7, 1895.

Feature: Celebrity Cyclists
p. 26: Belva Lockwood: "Belva Mounts Her Pegasus," *Washington Post*, March 7, 1882, in *Belva Lockwood: The Woman Who Would be President* by Jill Norgren, New York, New York University Press, 2007; p. 27: Annie Oakley: "Miss Annie Oakley: An Interview with the Little Cycling 'Sure Shot,'" *The Cycle Record*, September 3, 1892.

Chapter 2: "The Devil's Advance Agent"
pp. 28, 30: Charlotte Smith: "Is Bicycling Immoral? Woman's Rescue League Says It Is," *Brooklyn Eagle*, August 19, 1896; p. 30: Walsh: "The Rev. Dr. A. Stewart Walsh Replies to the Rescue League," *Brooklyn Eagle*, August 20, 1896; pp. 30-31: Ellen B. Parkhurst: "Plea for Wheelwomen: Charlotte Smith Is Wrong," *The Evening Times*, Washington, D.C., November 5, 1896; p. 32: Charlotte Smith: *Boston Globe*, August 31, 1896, quoted in *Raising More Hell and Fewer Dahlias: The Public Life of Charlotte Smith, 1840-1917*, by Autumn Stanley, Lehigh University Press, Bethlehem, Pennsylvania, 2009; Morphine: "Cycling Versus Morphine," *British Medical Journal*, November 30, 1895; p. 33: Dr. William C. Krauss: "Dangers of Bicycling; With Report of a Case of Acute Dilation of the Heart," by William C. Krauss, M.D., *Journal of the American Medical Association*, October 10, 1896; Dr. Benjamin Ward Richardson: "What To Avoid in Cycling," by Benjamin Ward Richardson, M.D., *The North American Review*, August 1895; p. 35: E.B. Turner: "A Report on Cycling in Health and Disease: IV. Cycling for Women," by E.B. Turner, *British Medical Journal*, June 6, 1896; p. 36: Joseph Bishop: "Social and Economic Influence of the Bicycle," by Joseph B. Bishop, *Forum*, Volume 21, 1896, p. 683; Charlotte Smith: "Is Bicycling Immoral? Woman's Rescue League Says It Is," *Brooklyn Eagle*, August 19, 1896; p. 39: Bishop: Bishop, p. 682; Maria E. Ward: *Bicycling for Ladies* by Maria E. Ward, New York: Brentano's, 1896.

Feature: Cycling Slang
p. 41: Bicycle Face: *Minneapolis Tribune*, July 20, 1895, quoted in Smith, p. 70.

Chapter 3: Fashion Forward
pp. 43-44: "The wind was behind me..." "Dress Reform Needed," *Sporting Life*, October 31, 1891, p. 7; p. 46: "These ladies..." "Women's Rights Convention," *New York Times*, August 2, 1852; p. 48: Amelia Jenks Bloomer: From an article by Amelia Bloomer in *Ladies Home Journal* reprinted in "The Rational Dress Movement, A Symposium," *The Arena* 9 (1893). Cited in *When the Girls Came Out to Play: The Birth of American Sportswear* by Patricia Campbell Warner, Amherst, Massachusetts: University of Massachusetts Press, 2006; pp. 49, 50: "Nearly two years ago..." "SHAME! The Sport Disgraced by the Antics of a Bloomerite," *Sporting Life*, October 14, 1893, p. 6; p. 50: Mrs. Reginald de Koven: "Bicycling for Women, by Mrs. Reginald de Koven, *The Cosmopolitan*, August 18, 1895; p. 50: A. F. W. Reimer: "Object to Women Bicyclists," *New York Times*, June 15, 1895; p. 53: "Some of the most valuable...": "Among the Wheelmen," *New York Times*, June 30, 1895; Caption: Paper doll by Gösta Kraemer, Pope Manufacturing Company, 1895; p. 54: "Women are too anxious...": "The Outdoor Woman," *Harper's Bazar*, May 2, 1896.

Feature: Cycling Songs
pp. 56-57: Sheet music lyrics for "Daisy Bell," "Get Your Lamps Lit!" and "Melissy" are available at JScholarship: Levy Sheet Music Collection, at Johns Hopkins University: *https://jscholarship.library.jhu.edu/handle/1774.2/2085*; Lyrics for the chorus of "Salute My Bicycle!" appear on the cover of its sheet music.

Chapter 4: Fast and Fearless
p. 58: "champion lady bicyclist of the world": "The Wheel," *Sporting Life*, January 27, 1886, p. 8; pp. 58, 61: "When an assistant...": "Only Six Laps Apart," *St. Paul Daily Globe*, December 24, 1886; p. 60, Caption: "Miss von Blumen's style...": "Hattie Still Leads: She Makes It Exciting at the Female Bicycle Race," *Pittsburg Dispatch*, January 4, 1889, p. 6; p. 61: Elsa von Blumen: *The Bicycling World*, December 16, 1881, p. 11, quoted in "Ordinary Women: High Wheeling Ladies in Nineteenth Century America," by S. Michael Wells, *Wheelmen Magazine*, November 1993; pp. 63-64: Quotations about Minneapolis race contestants: "Ladies Who Ride," *St. Paul Daily Globe*," April 26, 1891, and "Begins To-Morrow," *St. Paul Daily Globe*, May 3, 1891; p. 64: "in all probability...": "They Start To-Night," *St. Paul Daily Globe*, May 5, 1891; "rode like a wild woman...": "Nelson Still Leading," *St. Paul Daily Globe*, May 10, 1891; p. 67: "Men go to see...": "Now They're Off," *St. Paul Daily Globe*, May 6, 1891; p. 70: Dora Rinehart: From *The Cycling West*, quoted in "One for the Road," by Jeffrey Oliver, *5280 Magazine*, July 2006, p. 185; "long rides," "rain blizzards," and "She is an intellectual student...": "America's Greatest Cyclienne," *The Cycling West*, April 15, 1897; Dora Rinehart: Oliver, p. 182; Caption: *The Cycling West* quoted in "One for the Road," p. 183; p. 71: "America's Greatest Cyclienne"; "Miss Yatman plainly showed...": "Miss Yatman's Great Ride," *New York Times*, September 21, 1899; pp. 71, 73: "useless and..." and "Bitter rivalry...": "Mrs. Lindsay's 800 Miles," *New York Times*, October 19, 1899; "This ensures...": *Sporting Life*, January 18, 1896, p. 4; "No race meeting...": Constitution and By-laws of the League of American Wheelmen, 1897; "improper, immoral, and illegal...": "Police Stop Miss Gast," *New York Times*, October 20, 1900.

Feature: The Cycling Press
p. 74: "the largest...": "Cycling Papers," *Printers' Ink*, June 24, 1896, p. 18; p. 75: "the only weekly...": "Cycling Papers," p. 19; "The Bicycling Authority..." and "instructive and interesting articles...": "Announcement," *The Wheelwoman*, November 1895.

Chapter 5: New Freedoms
p. 77: "wonderful new style...": "The Era of the Bicycle" by Elizabeth Cady Stanton, *The American Wheelman*, May 30, 1895; p. 78: Frances Willard: *How I Learned To Ride the Bicycle* by Frances E. Willard, Sunnyvale, CA: Fair Oaks Publishing Company, 1991, pp. 73-74. Originally published as *A Wheel Within a Wheel*, 1895; p. 79: Frances Willard: Willard, pp. 74-75; "She possessed...": "Death of Miss Willard," *New York Times*, February 28, 1898; Caption: Willard, p. 27; p. 80: Frances Willard: Willard, p. 32; pp. 80-81: Ann Strong: *Minneapolis Tribune*, August 17, 1895, quoted in Smith, p. 81; p. 81: "The bicycle has brought..." "Women and the Bicycle," *L.A.W. Bulletin and Good Roads*, December 2, 1898, p. 405; Caption: "The Era of the Bicycle" by Stanton; pp. 81-82: "If she has ridden...": "Woman and the Wheel," *Munsey's Magazine*, May 1896, p. 159; p. 83: "Wheels and Wheels," by Madeline S. Bridges, *Outing*, September 1893, p. 460; pp. 83,84: "A Century Ride," by Grace E. Denison, *Outing*, October 1893, pp. 56-61; "A Fin de Cycle Incident," by Edna C. Jackson, *Outing*, June 1896, pp. 192-198. Reprinted in *The American 1890s* by Susan Harris Smith & Melanie Dawson, Editors, Durham, North Carolina: Duke University Press, 2000.

Highlights in Cycling and Women's History
p. 90: 1776: Abigail Adams's letter written March 31, 1776. Available at *thelizlibrary.org/suffrage/abigail.htm*.

INDEX

picture credits

acknowLedgments

As I set out to do the research for this book, I quickly learned one thing: People are passionate about bicycles. There are scores of collectors of vintage bikes and bicycle ephemera, and even more blogs and Web sites dedicated to all aspects of cycling. One site that's worth browsing is *Tubulocity.com*, an online magazine whose publisher, Eric Shalit, provided me with a crucial introduction to Dottie Batho. Dottie is the guardian of the Norman Batho Collection, an impressive compilation of thousands of vintage ads, cigar box labels, trading cards, pieces of sheet music, and more, all featuring bicycles. Her late husband Norman built the collection with great care, and Dottie was kind enough to give me access to it for this book.

Dottie also told me about the annual bicycle auction that takes place every April in Copake, New York (see copakeauction.com), which I attended with some success (though I stopped myself from bidding on the antique safeties and ordinaries). There, I met Beth Emery, a collector of historic images of women and bicycles who invited me to see her rare materials and ultimately let me use some of them. I am indebted to Eric, Dottie, and Beth, as well as to Peter Zheutlin, author of *Around the World on Two Wheels*, who provided me with a photograph of his great-grandaunt, "Annie Londonderry."

As always, my friends at National Geographic were invaluable collaborators, led by executive editor Jennifer Emmett, illustrations editor Lori Epstein, art director Jim Hiscott, and brilliant (and patient) designer Marty Ittner. Thanks also to my agent, Ken Wright; my parents, Ruth and Morris Macy; and my brother, Buddy Macy, for their encouragement and support, and to Jackie Glasthal for being there every step of the way.

Since 1888, the National Geographic Society has funded more than 12,000 research, exploration, and preservation projects around the world. The Society receives funds from National Geographic Partners, LLC, funded in part by your purchase. A portion of the proceeds from this book supports this vital work. To learn more, visit www.natgeo.com/info.

For more information, please call 1-800-647-5463 or write to the following address:

National Geographic Partners
1145 17th Street N.W., Washington, D.C. 20036-4688 U.S.A.

Visit us online at www.nationalgeographic.com/books

For librarians and teachers: www.ngchildrensbooks.org

More for kids from National Geographic: kids.nationalgeographic.com

For information about special discounts for bulk purchases, please contact National Geographic Books Special Sales: ngspecsales@ngs.org

For rights or permissions inquiries, please contact National Geographic Books Subsidiary Rights: ngbookrights@ngs.org

Printed in Hong Kong
16/THK/1